Robert Higgs is a graduate of Leeds Metropolitan University, a qualified Personal Trainer (YMCA) and an ABA Assistant Boxing Coach. He has been involved in various sports since the age of seven, weight training since the age of thirteen and has trained in boxing for the past three years.

This is his first book based on his experiences of bullying at school, and is an account of his success in rebuilding his life and confidence.

Robert has recently been invited to join The Royal Court Theatre's Young Writers Programme to help him develop his stage play, 'Watching The Parade Go By'.

He is currently working on his next three books and has a script, based on this book, in development.

WHAT HAVE I
EVER DONE TO YOU

Robert Higgs

What Have I
Ever Done To You

Pegasus

A CIP catalogue record for this title is
available from the British Library
ISBN 1 903490 08 1

*Pegasus is an imprint of
Pegasus Elliot MacKenzie Publishers Ltd.*

www.pegasuspublishers.com

First Published in 2002

**Pegasus
Sheraton House Castle Park
Cambridge England**

Printed & Bound in Great Britain

Dedication

This book is dedicated with love to the
great memories of my Nan and Grandad

Mrs D M Price & Mr F W J Price
xx

Acknowledgements

I would like to say a big thank you to author and self protection expert, Jamie O'Keefe of New Breed Publishing. Thank you Jamie for taking what was a 10 page manuscript and encouraging me to develop it into the book you are now reading.

Thank you also to: Tim Bartlett, Reuben Cole, Emma Higgs, 'Cheeky Gav' Jasper, Dan Newbould, Geoff Thompson, Dave Turton and Nigel White for the excellent interviews that add so many different perspectives to this book.

And finally thank you so much to: Howard Cardinal, Aidan Dunbar, David Higgs, Gareth Moseley, Chris Swanwick, Pilly Vidal, Sarah Walley, Mum, Dad and Uncle Trev for all your help and encouragement. May you all achieve your dreams in life.

Bullying

By Rob Higgs

Being bullied makes your school life hell
I can see the pain in your eyes where the tears well
Bullying makes you feel all alone
Living and breathing for the bell so you can go home.

But there's a better way to live your life
Your future isn't going to be all tears and strife
So don't panic when the fear comes in
Learn to control it, don't let it win

Deal with your worries
Because you haven't got the time
Life goes in a hurry
You need to change your mind

What the bullies say and do is rude
But you just need to change your attitude
Inside us all is a spirit so strong
Bullies are weak, believe me, you've done nothing wrong

Bullies love to stand and shout
But you must find the courage to let their secret out
Don't sit and take it without a sound
Look to yourself, friends, parents, teachers, help is all
around

So face your fears
And live your dreams
Don't stand for being bullied
It's really not as hard as it may seem

Chapter 1

Why A Book On Bullying?

I remember being five years old at school. One dinnertime I recall being offered the choice between being thrown into the stinging nettles or having my fingers bent back by a gang of five older lads. The question I asked then has become the title of this book – 'What Have I Ever Done To You?'

My book therefore is for the benefit of every person suffering from a lack of confidence that leaves them at the mercy of bullies. In Britain this accounts for an awful lot of people. Facts I obtained from BBC Online reveal that 1.3 million children a year are involved in bullying. A 1994 Sheffield University study disclosed that each week 350,000 primary school children and 100,000 secondary school children are victims of bullies. According to BBC Online, Bullying is also responsible for 30-50% of stress-related illness in the British workplace. The estimated annual loss is 80 million working days and £2 billion in revenue. Bullying also affects us in our homes; BBC Online estimates that 53% of adults are verbally or physically bullied by their partners.

Bullybeware.com estimates that in Britain someone is bullied every seven minutes, for an average of thirty seven seconds. It is also noted in schools that 71% of teachers claim to have intervened successfully in bullying. However only 25% of students report receiving effective help. Bullying is everywhere in our society; only most of it is brushed under the carpet and never comes to light.

And there you were thinking you were all alone, that it was only you in the whole world who was being victimised! I want you, the victim, to realise that you have the power and responsibility to build your confidence by facing your fears and leaving the 'victim state'. I wrote this book for you in the hope that you may see some similarity between my experience and your present situation. If so, I hope you will find information in this book that will change your life. The message I want to get across is that you must find your own way of solving the situation.

You may try different solutions and find that physically fighting off the bully is the only way they'll leave you alone. Some people may condemn you for that; you may get into trouble at school. But I urge you to do whatever it takes to stop the bullying. The simple fact is that bullying can and does destroy lives. It will destroy your life if you do not take action to stop it. It doesn't matter what anyone else thinks or says, you are the victim, the one going through it and you need to stop it in any way that you can.

Please take into account that I am not an academic or a psychologist with a million theories on the whys and wherefores of bullies and victims. What I am, though, is a young man who's been in the situations you're in and a young man who's lived the life you are presently living. I've been there and if you'll forgive the cliché, I've bought the T-shirt. I've seen bullying through the eyes of the victim. I understand because they were my eyes I was looking out of. I know that victims do not see bullying through rose-tinted spectacles. I also know that life doesn't have to be this way. There are answers to bullying and that's what this book is about.

I must say that having written this book I struggled

with many negative thoughts over whether I should actually try to get it published. I was ever so slightly ashamed at my former weaknesses and the things I allowed people to get away with. Perhaps it was just me that had experienced bullying I thought. However on a train journey one day I was presented with a powerful reason to publish my work.

The train pulled into the station to see a gang of young lads hanging around with their bottles of cider, cigarettes and bad haircuts. A similar looking lad got on the train and sat down. As he did one of the cider drinkers walked up to the carriage window, pointed to the lad and mouthed his threats of violence. The message registered with the lad on the train and his head dropped down to the floor with a look of utter sadness in his eyes.

That was it. I knew that expression; I'd worn that expression like a favourite coat. It's an expression that pleads 'Help me, I can't handle this.' It's an expression that the bully feeds on like a favourite snack. The message you convey is that your fear is in control and that you feel worthless. You search the room for anyone in the vicinity with a friendly face who can pull you away from your feelings.

I know because without need of a mirror I'd seen that look on my face a thousand times before. I felt pity for this teenage lad and felt angry at the cider drinker's behaviour. I was suddenly given the determination and conviction to get this book into print for all the people who need the advice.

I want to inspire you into such a state of determination that you will never again allow the 'victim state' a place in your body language. I want you to look into the mirror and instead see a confident and happy expression staring back at you.

The information within this book is demonstrative of

the fact that a person's past does not have to limit the potential and happiness of their future. The unhappiness I allowed myself to experience in my teens has not continued to be my life experience because I no longer allow it to be.

Through all the threats, barracking and putdowns I was always a heartbeat away from completely turning my life around. A lack of understanding of myself prevented me from standing up to the bullies. Today I have the knowledge that I was so desperately in need of a few short years ago, the knowledge that would have solved my problems and saved me years of unhappiness.

And now that I have this knowledge I feel it is my responsibility to pass it on. I am excited at the possibilities it holds for you, should you be willing to listen and learn from a young man who knows the bully/victim relationship from first-hand and painful experience. The opinions in the book are my own and based upon my own experiences. My experiences may be different from yours because each case of bullying is individual and personal to the victim.

However I am confident that you will gain inspiration from this book. If you are currently frightened of bullies and dread every new day at school then I have experience you can learn from. What I have to say may seem harsh or be a bitter pill to swallow but it is the truth as I have come to understand it.

If reading the book inspires you to positive action against the bullies in your life then I admire you very much. Some of the people that inhabit our world seem to exist only to make others unhappy. The truth however, is that they can only do so with YOUR consent and permission.

So for those of you lying in a darkened room, drenched by the downpour of sadness and depression...

your time is coming. For those of wallowing in the company of loneliness and for those of you who can't see the sunshine for the clouds… your time is coming. For those of you who feel sick with fear and worry or for those of you who wear your anger like a straitjacket… your time is coming.

Your time is the life YOU want to live and the person YOU want to become. So cultivate your courage and determination. Don't be scared of feeling scared. If you don't feel scared then there can be no courage. This is the start of a new beginning for you. The clock is ticking. Your time starts now.

Chapter 2

What Is Bullying?

My personal analogy of bullying is of the bully sinking in quicksand. They are up to their neck and both they and their self-esteem are sinking fast. In a desperate bid to escape they grab a victim, pulling them into the quicksand (or bully/victim relationship) as well. The bully then pushes the victim down under the sand in order to escape. Bullying is everywhere in our society. Bullies are girls, boys, men and women. They work either individually or in groups. They seek out people who give them what they want. Bullies thrive upon the victim.

Bullying is a form of relationship. All relationships involve communication. What is communication? Communication is the exchange of information between people. If the communication is not effective and there is no interaction between people then the relationship does not exist.

In my opinion all problems in relationships come from a lack of communication. The husband or wife, for example who comes home from work stressed and is moody and uncommunicative, causes tension because the other person doesn't know what's wrong and it leads to arguments. The only reason the bully and victim have a relationship is because the victim is presently unable to communicate in a way that will stop the bully's behaviour.

The Rules of The Game

The bully is only able to play the game because the victim is unable to defend themselves. The bully knows this yet continues to attack and cause harm. The bullies are therefore weak themselves because they will only pick on those who will play the game with them. The bully orders you to play the game. The rules are the bully's rules – whatever they say goes. If they say, for example, 'you're a w**ker,' then you've got to signal your agreement. These are the rules; the great thing is that if you don't like these rules (and who does?) then you don't have to play.

In the book '*Cat's Eye*' written by Margaret Atwood the main character Elaine, is bullied throughout her childhood by Cordelia. She tries for years to gain Cordelia's approval but it's never available. For years she plays the game by Cordelia's rules. One day the bullying stops though. It stops when Elaine decides she doesn't like the rules and doesn't want to play the game any more. Elaine walks away from Cordelia, ignoring the orders to 'come back here now'. Elaine leaves the game and is never bullied again.

In order for a bully to succeed they need the victim to communicate effectively with them. When a bully pushes you or threatens you or even tries to stare you out they are opening communications with you. The bully is asking you a question either verbally, through body language or actions. The question is always 'Will you let me bully you? Because if you're going to stand up to me I'm not interested'. Bullying revolves around this single question. When you do an exam you revise facts and prepare an answer to a certain question that you're expecting to be on the exam paper. If you revise well you will easily have a good answer when that question comes up, won't you?

However if you don't prepare yourself for that exam

question then you won't have an answer, or will get it wrong. It's the same with bullying. For many victims they simply don't know how to communicate the answer 'NO I won't let you bully me' or don't believe that giving such an answer will work. As a result they keep answering 'yes' and the bullying continues.

My aim in this book is to give you ideas as to how you can train yourself to communicate that 'NO' and to make the bully receive the message loud and clear.

Chapter 3

Life is very short

'Life is very short and there's no time for
fussing and fighting, my friend.'
The Beatles

The plight of both the victim saddens me greatly because bullying needn't go on. In his book 'Awaken the giant within' Personal Success Coach Anthony Robbins says that compared to the size of the universe the human life span is just a speck of dust in time. So why anyone would want to waste any of this time intimidating and victimising others is beyond me. I feel pity for the bullies that are wasting their time in a life that is a gift. In a similar way to cigarette smokers, bullies give away time from their lives with each incident. They are hurting themselves, but also hurting those they pick on in the process.

However by allowing bullies to influence our lives we are also losing valuable time. Think of all the fun you could be having if you weren't wasting time letting someone make you feel small. The time that you give away playing the role of a victim is not recoverable. Time is arguably the most valuable gift we have in life, once gone it cannot be regained. Today will never come again, the time you spend today pursuing your interests will never again exist in the same form. You have to make the most of this time and this is difficult to do when you're trapped in a bully/victim relationship. It doesn't matter whether your interests are in music, sports or the flight paths of bees. You will not get all the enjoyment out of them when you know that someone will make your life hell at school the next day. I hope that after reading this book you will stop the bullying in your life and start enjoying all the time you have.

But before you can do this you need to understand the nature of the problem you face. In my opinion any school, work or home environment is similar to an ocean. The bullies in that ocean can be likened to sharks. When a shark or bully smells blood, it comes looking for you at feeding time. Bullies however do not snack on fish or even passing swimmers' legs. Instead they rely upon the victim's fear to nourish their fragile egos.

What Is A Bully?

A bully is defined by Webster's World Dictionary as 'A person who hurts, frightens or tyrannises over those who are smaller or weaker.'

The key words for me here are 'smaller' and 'weaker'. Bullies are not strong people, however big, confident and intimidating they seem they are weak people. They are weak because they need to pick on others to feel good about themselves. They will only pick on people they see as weaker than themselves, who will allow them to get away with it.

If you are perceived as having weaknesses then the bully will spot them and attack. If I can draw you an analogy, bullies at school act in the same way as a selection panel at a job interview. Bullies are very proficient at spotting those who might be suitable for employment. Unfortunately employment as a victim offers no job satisfaction, company car or dream salary.

Employment as a victim requires you to contribute your self-esteem to the bully. The bully in effect robs you of your self-esteem and uses it to bolster theirs. Like I said, there is no dream salary, in fact you're working for free. The bully is taking the wages or self-esteem that is rightfully yours. Being a victim of bullying therefore simply offers YOU the chance to be a punching bag for someone else's insecurities and vindictive nature.

The Victim:

A hypothetical job advert seeking a victim might therefore read as follows:

Person wanted: Victim of bully.
Necessary qualities: Passive, feels paralysed by fear, will not fight back, feels overwhelmed by the situation.

You must accept that you will only be 'offered the job' if you are seen to have the necessary qualities. If you don't and make it clear to the bully that you are not available then he will not be able to 'employ' you.

The bully will screen every pupil's behaviour in the school environment. In each class, at each break and lunchtime, in the changing rooms or on the sports field. Even on the way to and from school the bully is keeping an eye out for potential victims. The bully has a need to pick on someone like an alcoholic needs a drink. When they find someone who seems suitable they think 'Great!' It's like winning the lottery or going home and finding their favourite meal on the table for them. When you're in their sights they move in for the kill.

So what exactly is a victim?

A victim is defined by Webster's World Dictionary as 'Someone who is killed, destroyed, injured or otherwise harmed by or suffering from some act, condition or circumstance.' If YOU'RE being bullied then that victim is YOU.

What I want to do here is describe to you exactly what a victim state is and why it makes you a target for bullying. Reaching an understanding of this will show you how to change it; after all you can't extinguish a fire in a building until you find out where it is. Doing this will make you less likely to stand out in a crowd as a potential victim to a bully. It is a persons 'Victim state' that allows the bullying to go on. So what forms can bullying actually take? Here are the three forms of bullying I have had experience of:

1. Physical

This involves being pushed, pulled, grabbed, punched or kicked. This form cuts to the chase and involves a physical attack upon your person. It may also involve people pushing in front of you in queues, taking your belongings off you, locking you in rooms and other intimidatory tactics like following you home. If you have a bike they might ride alongside you or try to push you off it.

2. Mental

This centres on being teased, taunted or challenged by others. The taunts may be about your clothes, shoes, friends etc. Some bullies will even deliberately call you by the wrong name just to annoy you. It might even happen just because you're there or because you've got something the bully hasn't. Very often it will involve threats of attack or physical violence e.g. 'I'm gonna kick your f**kin' head in.' This was something I got a lot of at school, people threatening to knock me down, beat me up or in the local vernacular, 'twat me one.' Although I don't remember anyone actually following up on their threats.

To be honest the only reason this bothered me so much at the time was because I thought I was a wimp for not fighting and for walking away. The truth is that I wasn't at all, I didn't want to fight and I didn't need to. My attitude has changed now and people can try and threaten me all they like, as long as I don't feel they really will attack me I don't have to fight them. I will walk away every time because I've got better things to do. In addition to this you may (as my sister did) get abusive or threatening phone calls from bullies. The threats may be of another kind, at school aged five my friendly bully would threaten to get me into trouble with the police (his dad was a police officer).

3. Relational

This is where a person is rejected or excluded by a group, when everyone else is accepted. This happened to me when I was about fourteen with one of my best friends at the time. We both played golf at the local club and always went round together. My friend was ever so slightly temperamental and after every bad shot or missed putt, he'd almost wrap his golf club around himself in his rage. I got fed up with the constant effort of trying to keep him calm and enjoy playing so I suggested we went around with other people rather than just us two.

I was also ambitious as usual and wanted to really improve my game and knew that playing with people better than me would help me do it. My friend didn't take kindly to the suggestion and for the next few months at the club, he ignored me and refused to speak to me. Two other lads also joined the club who we both were friends with and this lad convinced them to ignore me as well. I would walk onto the tee just as they were leaving and they wouldn't speak or ask me to join them. I was again left stupidly thinking I'd done something wrong. The only mistake I did make was to seek the friendship of someone with less control over his emotions than Happy Gilmore. Relational bullying may also take the form of bullies deliberately ignoring you when you talk to them as if you're not worth talking to.

Any weakness or insecurity you have as a victim will be picked out and highlighted by the bullies. Whatever weakness you have will be used to bully you and make you feel small. If you're not too confident about your physical appearance, if you feel too fat, too skinny, too tall or too short and you have negative feelings about it the bullies will pick up on it. They will insult you, see you are upset but unwilling to do anything about it and the bullying will begin.

If you are afraid of fighting and confrontation you will be challenged and intimidated. We all have insecurities and bullies can pick them out, but if you are not upset and do not seek the approval of others then you will not bully yourself. If we do not bully yourself then the bullies will have less chance of hurting you. Whether the bullying is physical, mental or relational the important thing to remember is that bullying in any form is an attack on your person and is very wrong.

A victim may experience one or even all three types at once. In my opinion though bullying on a mental level is far more painful an experience. This is because the threats play on an underdeveloped mind that is suffocated by fearful thoughts. Often the threats are not actually carried out which causes more damage to the victim who is forever waiting in anticipation for a beating that never arrives. The bully understands that if there is no actual violence it will keep the victim scared. After all if the bully hit you and despite your fear you realised he wasn't as tough as you thought. Then you're likely to lose your fear and the bully will no longer have an ego-boosting victim.

The bully wants you to keep playing the game and it's your fear and insecurity that allows it to continue. The bully doesn't want bullying you to be hard work. He or she wants victimising you to be easy. That's why they employ targeting and a feeling out stage. The bully will notice whatever weakness you have that leaves you open to being a victim. Someone may be successful in bullying you, for example, because you are held back by a fear of fighting. Surely it is preferable to actually have a fight and discover that it wasn't so scary after all than forever live in nervous anticipation of getting beaten up? The result of never actually fighting back leaves the victim in a permanent state of self-doubt as to whether they actually could succeed. The self-doubt spills over into every area of your life, which is why I believe mental bullying is far more damaging to your psyche.

Whatever form the treatment does take however I have discovered that Bullying will last as long as YOU allow it to and it's as simple as that. A bully will only select a victim who is unlikely to fight back. The bully's behaviour is caused by personal weakness. The bully though is not your enemy and you should feel no hatred towards him or her. You may not realise this but your real enemy is not the idiot in front of you in a blazer and tie. In fact I think sometimes bullying is inadvertent. Perhaps sometimes people don't realise they are upsetting us or at times we don't realise that what we are doing is upsetting them. But whatever the reason you need to realise that you don't have to endure bullying, there are solutions to the problem.

As a victim your real enemy, the enemy you have to stand up to and fight is the FEAR and NEGATIVITY IN YOUR OWN MIND. These two factors are what produce the 'Victim State.' You can train yourself to deal with these thoughts and feelings. Then you can replace them with thoughts and feelings of courage, self-esteem, pride, confidence and positivity. In doing this you will become mentally strong. When you are mentally strong you will convey that strength sub-consciously to anyone you meet. When you are mentally strong the bully will think twice before selecting you as a victim because you will no longer be displaying a victim's characteristics. In fact with all the training you'll have done the very idea of allowing yourself to be bullied again should be enough to make you sick.

At present though, you are a victim and passive in certain situations, under the control of your own negative thoughts. You may be painfully shy and withdrawn at school; you may walk with your head down to avoid catching anyone's gaze. It's likely you are passive and apologetic because you don't want to make anyone angry with you. A low opinion of your self worth will also likely be a part of your makeup. Whatever the effects on your personality I'm sure you will agree that being bullied holds you back in your life.

Whenever I was picked on I accepted it because my own mind bombarded me with negative thoughts that told me I could do nothing about it. It began really at the age of twelve when I had to move house and schools.

I had been respected and free of bullying at my previous schools but the new one involved starting again. I went there feeling scared because I didn't know anyone in the new place. The new environment was one I was totally unprepared for. The kids spoke a different language at this school and most of the words began with an F or a C.

I was very keen obviously to make friends and some kids took advantage of that. People began to test me to see how I would react to certain comments. They wanted to know how far they could push me. Was I a fighter or was I game for anyone who wanted an ego boost by picking on me? This question always seemed to be answered for people by watching you fight for the first time. Although I won my first fight I think people saw that my fighting skills were nothing to be afraid of. I certainly was not a threat to the school's renowned fighters. Once people saw this they got braver at testing me out. Being shy I did not answer the insults and threats for fear of having to fight and my confidence got lower and lower like a limbo dancer.

I had to work hard to break into the football and rugby teams. Perhaps some of the kids were threatened by this or annoyed that some new kid had taken their mate's place. But from this point on for about four years people would go out of their way to tell me I was crap at the sports I played so well. They highlighted my weaknesses and ignored my successes. Another golfing story of mine illustrates this well. When I joined the golf club a lad from school was acknowledged as being an excellent player (and he was). His dad used to watch him in competitions and if he saw me he'd always offer encouragement, until that is I beat his son fair and square at golf.

All I heard at school was 'I hear you've joined the golf club, you'd never beat him, he says you're crap.' It was even the subject of conversation in class one day. I said I was improving, everyone else bar none said I was crap and that he'd beat me. After a while we did have a game, my handicap was twenty shots higher than his (making him the better player), so I should by rights have been given shots to make it fairer. Instead I asked to play him level and I beat him fair and square. Instead of shaking my hand he stormed off up the fairway as if his shoes were on fire, leaving me to walk in on my own. Neither he nor his dad were ever friendly or encouraging to me again.

One career bully picked on me for about four years. He was and probably still is a bully. In fact we'd played against each other at mini-rugby a couple of years before I moved to this lad's area. He was sent off that day for punching our scrum half. When I later played on the same team he was regularly sent off for fighting. I have tried to work out why he singled me out, but I can honestly say that I never said or did anything that could have caused him to dislike me.

I was a talented rugby player and about a year after moving house I was asked by a mate to play for the local rugby club. The bully was on the same team and I was told he wasn't happy about me coming to play for his team. Apparently he'd tried to convince everyone that I was rubbish, but a lot of people had told him I was the better player (which wound him up). We played in different positions but both were good at placekicking.

My skill at this was coming to the attention of the coach and I guess the bully realised I was challenging him. Once after we'd scored a try I asked him if I could take the conversion kick, he showed me his insecurity by grabbing the ball and telling me to F off. Eventually though he had a bad game and I was given the kicking duties. He never got them back, which didn't make me his favourite person.

He was also apparently outraged when I told one of the other lads on the team that my ambition was to play for England. I've always believed that any talents I have can be developed by hard work. Many times I have developed skills in areas that I have no natural talent for, so I believed I had a shot at one day playing for England. He let me know what he thought about that at an area rugby training session. I was tackled to the floor and set the ball up for a ruck. Everyone rushed in and I got a boot right in the mouth, when I looked up I saw the bully standing over me.

A couple of years later I was training in the gym when he came in with the same mate who'd told him of my England plans. By this time I'd developed my body a lot and was able to train at an advanced level for my age. I noticed that I was actually physically stronger now than the bully. He sent his mate over to tell me that I wasn't doing the exercise properly and that if I did it his way, with the same weight, I would find it more difficult (I didn't). At the time it made me angry but now it just makes me laugh. I can't believe these people went to such lengths to put me down.

If I could draw you an analogy to sum up my bullied existence, it was like tuning into a radio station that played all the songs I didn't like. Instead of changing the station I allowed myself to listen to the same tunes again and again. In response I used to let people put me down but try to ignore it. Although it made me angry I just bottled it up. Constantly feeling anger eventually dragged me down into depression.

What I needed to do and what YOU need to do now is turn the radio station off altogether. Don't just try to turn the volume down. Turn it off completely and never listen to it again I could regale you with detailed tales of bullying and how it made me feel sad, withdrawn and depressed. I could advise you to seek counselling and pour out your

33

feelings of woe. But the simple truth is that Bullying will last as long as you allow it to and it's as simple as that. This book is about honesty and understanding yourself. When you understand yourself and the reason why you allow bullies power, you can train yourself to be strong.

To accomplish this YOU must train your mind and the thoughts you allow within it. Make your thoughts strong and positive. Armed with these thoughts you won't allow yourself to be victimised next time the bullies decide to boost their egos on you. Be determined to kick bullying out of your life. Make this new perception of yourself reality and you will be on the road to a happier life. Life is meant to be a treat not a trial. Listen to John Lennon's words in the song *Instant Karma*, 'So why on earth are we here? Surely not to live in pain and fear!' So waste no more time being unhappy. This will require courage and discipline but as I have discovered the pain of this is significantly less than the pain of regret.

Chapter 4

The Bullying Ritual

From my own experience bullies follow a set ritual when selecting a victim. Like Arnold Schwarzenegger searching for Linda Hamilton in the film 'Terminator', a bully will scan the area for an available victim. Once the victim has been selected and targeted there is a feeling-out stage. Bullies you see are often cautious and insecure. They're similar to boxers trading feints instead of punches at the start of a bout. The bully, like the boxer wants to see how strong the intended victim is. They're not looking for an opponent; they're after someone who won't fight back.

Victim Targeting: Parallels With The Animal Kingdom.

In his book 'The Trials of Life' David Attenborough recounts the hunting ritual of cheetahs and dogs. He writes that cheetahs usually begin by 'stalking' a herd of gazelles. The cheetah will immediately pick out the weakest of the herd, the one seen 'grazing in an approachable position.' The cheetah will then break into a sprint and chase the gazelle. It generally either captures the gazelle in the first hundred yards or so. If it does not the cheetah will usually give up. Like a typical bully, the cheetah does not want to work too hard for its prey.

The bullying ritual begins with the bully selecting the most likely victim from a group. The bully will approach the victim and when sure they won't fight back, will attack verbally or physically. Basically the bully is looking for any excuse, (however flimsy) to pick on you. Generally if the victim offers any resistance at all the bully, like the cheetah will give up and wait for another victim.

Dogs though hunt gazelles in a slightly different manner. They chase the whole herd and different individual gazelles in order to establish which ones are least likely to outrun them. When they have found the weakest members they will pursue them exclusively. Some bullies will use this approach themselves. They may try the same comment or approach on different people in a group. Whoever is established, as the weakest will be the one who is picked on.

In my experience a bully will use either approach, depending on their confidence and prior knowledge of a group. After a few weeks in a certain class at school, a bully will know who the most confident people are and who the easy victims are. It depends upon the individual bully. Some may be like the cheetahs and will immediately select the weakest person in the class or group for abuse. Others may be like the dogs and will test numerous people in the group to find the people who will submit to bullying.

Eye Contact

Often a bully will select a potential victim and stare at them. If the victim's gaze drops to the ground it's a message the bully salivates at like one of Pavlov's dogs. This act of submission communicates to the bully that he or she can approach the victim for a spot of ego bashing.

Holding eye contact, though, could be seen by the bully as a challenge and could lead to a confrontation. It is perhaps better to look away to the side. But never look down because it is submissive. If you do this the bully will make a mental note that you are a potential victim. You should be aiming to gain confidence and avoid looking like a target to the bully. Therefore please be aware that eye contact is one way in which a bully is searching constantly for openings. The bully looks for weaknesses he can exploit in people.

When these are located the bully attacks and wins the game, making himself or herself feel good. That's what bullying is in reality: a game. It has its own set of rules and regulations. It's a game that cannot be played outside of these rules. It cannot be played on its own, the bully must have someone to 'play' with. The bully needs a certain set of circumstances. If these are not in place the game cannot be played.

The way a bully starts a relationship with a victim is remarkably similar to the process of attracting the opposite sex. A girl or boy might see you from across the room, for example. If they're attracted to you perhaps they'll make eye contact. Depending on their confidence they may wait for you to return eye contact or just approach you straight away. When they've approached you they'll get your attention with a conversation. Through the conversation and your body language the girl or boy will decide if they want to have further relations with you.

Once the victim has been targeted the game continues with the feeling-out stage.

Bullies are not strong people and need reassurance that the person targeted will play the role of the victim. They acquire this reassurance by gradually testing the water. However, bullies do not jump straight into the water, so to speak, in case it is scalding hot. This is too risky because they might get a punch in the eye for their trouble. Instead they gradually push you and test you until they're sure you won't fight back. Again the point at which they receive sufficient reassurance will depend on the individual bully and their confidence level.

If the bully went straight into smashing their fist into your face you'd have a clear message that they didn't like you. I'd say this would be easier to stop straight away. However when the bullying begins with subtle requests like 'Pass me that ball' or 'Lend us 50p' you may do so out of friendliness. Then without realising it you're already falling under their control. You've already obeyed a command and started down the unhappy road of obedience.

When the bullying is then stepped up a gear and the bully becomes aggressive the victim is already up the scaffolding without a ladder. It's like spending money on a credit card and being sent a huge bill at the end of the month. It can hit you hard if you've been acting out of friendliness and you're suddenly hit with aggression.

When I started a new school aged twelve I didn't know anyone and was understandably keen to make friends. By way of my own niceness and willingness to make friends I became a target. I was fair game for anyone who wanted to test the water with simple requests and comments. I realise now that from the first minute I entered that new classroom I was under the spotlight. I was being tested by the bullies to see if I was prone to being a victim and unfortunately for me; I was. Before I realised what was happening these people all were dominating me because I was at a new school and needed to make friends.

In retrospect I didn't confront people for fear of falling out with any prospective friends. Therefore I allowed the insults to continue in the hope that it was just banter and would eventually go away… it didn't.

'Am I really being bullied or is it just friendly banter?' is a question you may want answering. The simple guideline is to follow your own feelings and trust your own perception. A joke is only a joke if both the joker and the recipient enjoy it. If someone's behaviour towards you upsets you, angers you, then you need to confront people and tell them you won't stand for it.

When it comes to selecting victims and testing the water we can perhaps credit bullies with a certain amount of intelligence. We can't credit them with any courage because they need reassurance that the victim won't fight back before the bullying is stepped up. The bully needs to know that they can get away with it. Once you are firmly entrenched in the bully/victim relationship it becomes easy work for the bully. At lunchtime they know to visit the canteen for food. Similarly they know whom to visit when their ego needs boosting – YOU.

It isn't a challenge for the bully and that's why they are not 'hard' and are not deserving of respect. The only things holding the victim in his limited pattern of behaviour are fear, shame and a lack of confidence. Once this is remedied the victim will be in a position to confront the bully. They can watch amazed as the bully's invincible persona folds like paper in the hands of the world origami champion.

One of the very best examples of a bully testing the water (if you'll pardon the history lesson) is that of Hitler and the build up to World War Two.

The First World War had been the most destructive conflict known to man and had instilled a deep horror in most people of such a thing ever happening again. However the post-war settlement was vindictive and reduced the beaten German nation to a shadow of its pre-war self. Germany was forced to accept the blame for all the devastation, lost the ability to defend its people and had some of its territory taken away.

Hitler and his Nazi party came to power from a background of violence and intimidation of competing political parties. Once in power Hitler set about trying to recapture Germany's former power. He played upon the reluctance of the British and French governments to be drawn into further war. Hitler was a bully who found the necessary weaknesses by threatening force and recapturing Germany's lost territories.

He was also able to play on the guilt of Britain and France in enforcing such a vindictive settlement upon Germany (the Treaty of Versailles). This is similar to a victim who perhaps has had an experience that made them ashamed or guilty. Their self-esteem is lowered as a consequence and they are anxious to make concessions to make up for their mistake. In the bully/victim context Britain and France felt guilty and were keen to accede to Hitler's demands. Their shame and reluctance to stand up to Hitler was in effect their 'victim state'. And it was this that initially allowed Hitler so much success.

Hitler saw these weaknesses and pushed the two governments a little further each time until it became apparent that a war might ensue. He began with small requests and when these were obeyed he moved onto more aggressive demands. This is similar to a bully at school asking you to lend them a pen and then next time becoming more aggressive. These demands were backed up by the threat of war if Britain and France did not comply. Very similar to a bully saying, 'Close that door or I'll knock you out' isn't it?

Each success gave Hitler more time to rebuild the German armed forces and he became increasingly threatening. Britain and France did everything in their power to avoid a war. Had they confronted Hitler it is now thought that he would have backed down. The delay in doing this only served in giving Britain and France a more dangerous enemy to fight. Similarly, by feeding a bully's confidence you only make a confrontation more difficult for yourself. The worst case scenario for Britain and

France was a war and fear of this consequence motivated their acquiescence to Hitler's demands. The British Prime Minister flew out to meet Hitler on his terms to mediate and avoid conflict. He famously returned claiming he had secured 'peace in our time.'

Hitler then made new demands over Poland and Britain was forced to mediate again. In this case they gave Hitler, the bully, a warning. If he invaded Poland then Britain and France would declare war on Germany. This was in effect their 'fence', like in a self-defence situation when you keep a person at arms length and warn them to stay away from you.

The problem was that Britain and France, or the victim, was not taken seriously. They had backed down to Hitler, the bully, so many times that he did not believe their threat. The result of course was that Hitler invaded Poland and Britain and France had to fight for their own survival. It was a classic case of a solution to bullying. Do everything you can to resolve it peacefully but if someone is determined to fight you then you must fight back or be trampled under the bully's stamping feet.

Chapter 5

Bullying – The Victim's Responsibility

'Take away the cause and the effect ceases.'
Miguel de Cervantes.

Previously I said that as a victim, you have certain characteristics that mark you out as a target for bullies. However you are not the cause of the problem, the bully is. The bully is the cause and if they were taken out of the picture there wouldn't be anyone to pick on you. Take away the cause (i.e. the bully) and the effect (i.e. your unhappiness) will cease.

You are not responsible for the behaviour of your tormentor. You are not to blame and should not allow yourself or other people to make you feel it is in anyway your fault. If this person weren't bullying you they would probably be doing it to someone else. However I have called this chapter 'Bullying – the Victim's Responsibility' because you do have a responsibility. First you need to report the problem and secondly you need to increase your confidence so you're less of a target. The bully has behavioural problems that need dealing with by the proper authorities i.e. the schoolteachers.

Allowing the bullying to continue will have a very bad effect on the health of your body and mind. There are many solutions to the problem and many ways to make yourself less of a target. However it is vital and extremely brave to take the attitude that you won't allow it to happen any longer and that somehow you will find a way to stop it. The previous chapter will have demonstrated to you that your main problems are caused by the psychological effect of the bully's actions on you.

The 'victim state' must clearly be in evidence in order for the bully to get the reaction they want from their attack. This is the cause that allows the bully to achieve the desired effect. By training yourself to go into an assertive state when you are victimised rather than a passive one then you can stamp out the cause and consequently the effect. You need to cut the 'victim mentality' from your persona like a surgeon would a cancerous growth.

Think of it this way: a plant does not grow without seeds; a car does not go without petrol. Your 'victim state' is the fuel that allows the bully to dominate you. It is the necessary condition and circumstance for you to allow the bully to take away your power and batter your self-esteem. By taking responsibility you can learn to stop displaying 'victim' signals that create an opportunity for the bully's behaviour. Obviously you didn't ask to be bullied but you need to improve on the things about yourself that mark you out as a victim.

In my teenage 'victim state' I would walk by certain people hoping not to be spotted. When people would insult me I would get that nervous feeling in my stomach and would feel a deep sadness. At that time though I would not allow the anger I felt to come to the surface. With the bittersweet gift of hindsight I can see that when I asked for help and got none I should have taken the responsibility to train myself to fight. Unfortunately I did not until years later.

The three main mistakes I made that prolonged my suffering were as follows. Firstly I did not report my situation to anyone. Secondly, I did not answer back, and finally I did not fight back. The bullying I experienced was almost entirely through taunts and threats. People got to know through other people 'testing the water' that I would not retaliate for fear of fighting. Therefore I would capitulate and suffer in silence.

If challenged to fight I would lose the fight to my own mind because I allowed myself to be held down by my fear of being incapable of hitting hard enough to win the fight. Even in a very large school environment there is what is referred to as a 'pecking order'. (And I felt I occupied a low position in that order.)

Everyone in the school knows all the renowned fighters. Likewise everyone in the school knows the renowned 'victims'.

It's unfortunate but from day one in school everyone is under the microscope and observation of everyone else. Everyone is known for something. You have different labels for people: 'hard', 'wimp' or 'victim', 'clever/swot' or 'comedian', are the main ones. Being known as a 'victim' does leave you open to the approaches of the weak bullies who need to have that feeling of power over another person.

Each defeat I suffered at the hands of my own mind strengthened the grip the fear had over me and increased my reputation as a 'victim'. With each successive defeat it became harder and harder to consider the prospect of fighting back. My situation resembled a tent peg being gradually bashed into the ground with a mallet. I made the mistake of thinking the bullies had enormous power, I allowed my own mind to represent them as invincible. In reality it only appears so because the bully is in possession of your power. This is the power you currently feel unable to access because you are held back by your fears.

It is unfortunate that the world makes a home to those who seek to make you unhappy but as I said earlier people can only do this if you allow it. A bully can only succeed in making you miserable if you give them your consent and permission.

Imagine a piece of paper. On it are the words 'I consent to being treated by you in any way you like. Push, slap, kick, punch or even stamp on my head and spit on me but I promise not to resist.' Imagine a second piece of paper that reads 'OK, I'll do that until you decide to stop me.'

The first statement is written, signed and postmarked by YOU the victim. The bully writes the second piece. It really is like standing at the altar getting married. It's like a legally binding document that the victim is prevented from breaking by fear and shame. As a victim you're choosing to accept the terms. If you were married and your spouse treated you that way would you tolerate such a destructive relationship? Of course not. You'd want a divorce, right? Well, take responsibility for yourself right now and choose to divorce from the bully/victim relationship.

The opportunity is there for you. Don't allow the thoughts that tell you you're weak to occupy your mind. You will feel scared, you will want someone to help you, to take you away from the pain you feel. What you must embrace is the fact that you don't need anyone to do this. You can do it yourself. You are capable of doing it yourself and it's a great opportunity for you to develop confidence by doing it. Waiting and relying upon others to intervene will only slow your progress to a happier life. So commit totally to changing and go ahead and do it. When I went travelling around the world, I briefly met this middle-aged foreign guy in San Francisco. Despite it being almost 4.30am in the hostel lobby, he turned out to be a bit of a philosopher. I'd like to pass on what he said (and hope he doesn't ask for royalties).

'In life,' he said, 'don't think about what is impossible, think about what could be.' Don't allow yourself to see being bullied as an impossible situation. Picture in your head how you'd like your life to be and go make it happen.

It is natural and commonplace for the victim to feel at fault for being bullied. After a while you do start to feel that it's your fault and that you have something wrong with you. You may also feel guilty about something you've done that makes you feel deserving of the treatment. These thoughts are all natural and shared by millions of victims worldwide.

And in my opinion these thoughts account for a large percentage of bullying cases that go unreported. These thoughts grant the bully licence to carry on hurting you because in some way you feel responsible.

However when I talk about you having responsibility as a victim I'm talking about something different. The victim's responsibility is to report to those in authority, exactly what is going on and who has been involved in it. You are not the weak link in the chain with regard to bullying you see. Yes, you have a certain lack of confidence that allows the bully to target you. But the truth is that the bully is far weaker than you are. The bully is so weak that he, she or they need to make you feel small so they can feel good about themselves. They are so weak that they are afraid to pick on someone who will not stand for it. They have weaknesses that need help and weaknesses that will not allow them a happy life.

The bullies are the problem and they have caused problems in society for years and years. If the problem is ever going to dealt with, if society as a whole is ever going to progress, the bullies need to be reported. The problems they cause you and others must be dragged into the open. When I talk about your responsibility I'm asking you to be forward-thinking, look beyond your own situation and see an even bigger picture. You can play your part in creating a better society by shining a light on the weak behaviour of bullies. Individually, you may feel alone in your situation. However you are part of a collective of millions of people, of all ages and backgrounds who have been, and are being bullied. Therefore each victim has an individual responsibility to improve their life by reporting bullying. And they also have a collective responsibility to society and all the other victims to report bullying. People's fear and shame keeps brushing bullying under the carpet and hinders the road to a solution. I will say it once more in bold capitals and I hope you get it: BULLYING PLAGUES OUR SOCIETY; IT IS NOT THE VICTIM'S FAULT. Please accept your responsibility to bring your individual case into the open.

Chapter 6

Remaining A Victim – The Price You Pay

Allowing bullying to remain a part of your life more than a day longer will be an unnecessary delay to your happiness and will lead you to ill health. Remaining a victim of bullying is about as healthy as taking an axe and hacking off your head. It's also about as beneficial to your social life. When you start feeling paranoid, worthless, ashamed and unhappy you find yourself declining offers to go out. When you do go out you feel miserable and it's no fun. Your self-esteem gets battered to a ragged mess and years later you can still feel the effects.

When you want to interview someone you admire for your book, for example and they say yes. You recoil in shock because you can't believe they want to help you. It's the same when you meet a girl that turns your trousers into a tent at first sight and she wants to be with you. You think, 'well I haven't got any money, she must like me!'

Bullying can and will destroy your life. It had such a devastating effect on my self esteem that melancholy became a constant companion. The loss of confidence also made me paranoid and I became very quick to think that people didn't like me. I would get defensive when friends tried a bit of mickey taking and I became extremely prone to strange moods and irrational behaviour. I think I even lost a couple of friends because of this, which I'm sorry about. The happiness I have now was put on hold for many years. Since coming to terms with my experiences I've been playing catch up with all the things I missed out on in my teens.

Being bullied was an incredibly hard experience for me, but also an unnecessary one. Please accept that unhappiness will continue to be your life experience until you commit yourself to facing up to yourself and your fears. Doing this sooner rather than later will minimise the psychological damage you will suffer. Most of the damage done to you by bullying will be to your self-esteem.

Self Esteem

Your self-esteem is the regard you have for yourself and the level at which you value yourself as a person. Bullying does gradually erode that level of self-esteem. Think of the bullying being like a flu virus for example. The virus exhausts the body's ability to fight back. Your immune system becomes run down and you go into a state of illness. Your body has numerous cells that are there to keep you alive by fighting illness and its potential. When you get ill your body takes action to rid your body of the illness. You need to do the same with your life – get rid of the bullying.

You have attributes that can shield you from the harm done by bullies. These 'cells' or attributes are your confidence and self esteem. There was a cartoon character when I was a kid (not too long ago), called Batfink. His catchphrase used to be 'You can't hurt me. My wings are like a shield of steel.' If you make your self-esteem and confidence into a 'shield of steel,' you'll be impervious to a bully's attacks and nothing they say or do to upset you will work.

When such attributes are in short supply we do not have sufficient 'cells' to combat the stressor and we do get bullied or ill. If you allow bullying to break you down you will gradually lose your self-esteem and confidence in yourself. It is at this point that life really becomes a struggle. I know from experience that if you let this happen just getting yourself to go to school can become incredibly hard. I found a good example of the price of remaining a victim on the front page of The Daily Express (October 24th 2000) which ran the headline 'Bullied girl sues school for £75,000'. (One of the first cases of this happening.) The girl involved (named Leah) gave details on the psychological effects of bullying which are very useful here. She said she suffered from depression and 'post-traumatic stress disorder.' Leah had problems with sleeping, very low self-esteem, anxiety attacks and flashbacks of bullying incidents.

The problems began when she moved to a new school aged nine. Pupils started calling her 'prostitute' and 'swot'. The physical abuse came in the shape of being punched, poked and slapped. According to the report she was at one stage pushed into the path of an oncoming car while a large gang of kids stood and jeered. She said that the treatment was continuous and even led to the bullies throwing eggs at her house and writing obscene graffiti about her.

Leah reported that she had gone to the school dinner ladies for help but had been told, 'to stop telling tales'. To escape the torment she pretended to be ill to avoid going to school. The problems were compounded by the fact that she kept her anguish inside, eventually leading to a nervous breakdown. Leah is quoted as saying that going to school was like 'walking to an electric chair.'

In a similar report that day a pupil won £1500 in damages from his old school as a result of bullying that left him needing psychiatric treatment. The boy was called a 'lanky loner' when the bullying began in the form of verbal abuse. Apparently he kept a diary of his experiences and tried to tape the bully's comments on a dictaphone. The pupil eventually left the school having gone from being 'confident and popular to very withdrawn and quiet.' The article reports that at some point one third of girls and one quarter of boys are afraid to go to school because of bullying.

The Daily Express also ran an article on the 14th December 2000 in which the comedian Alan Davies recounted his experience of being bullied.

'When I was 12 I was picked on for weeks by a group of older lads, who would yank my tie or trip me up. It didn't go on for long but it was enough to make me depressed. After a while they moved onto someone else, someone of a different race or someone who they thought might be gay. I didn't want to go to school.'

I'm sure you'll agree that none of these cases make for happy reading. I do feel though that you can learn from the experiences of the above victims. Keeping the problems to herself after initially being rebuffed by the dinner ladies led Leah to a nervous breakdown. The second victim also required professional help after having his previously high self esteem trampled on.

What we are talking about here are people whose lives have been severely damaged by their experiences. The psychological scars do take a lot of time to heal, the interview with my sister Emma shows that 3-4 years on she still has difficulty representing her experiences in a positive light.

Each time you allow yourself to be bullied you make the pattern harder to break because you are training yourself to suffer in silence. If the bully has targeted you before you'll tend to go into the 'Victim State' on the bully's approach. Your shoulders will slump, your chin will drop and you will probably feel a wave of sadness and helplessness inside. Should you have to walk past the bully it's likely you'll look straight ahead, like a motorist driving past a police car on the motorway.

By remaining passive and keeping your anger at the bully inside you succeed only in damaging your internal organs and immune system. I often felt physically ill because of the anger I would not let out.

Self-Bullying

Everyone at some stage bullies themselves. How many times have you made a mistake and told yourself how stupid you were for doing it? Taking a punch or abusive comment off a bully and keeping your anger inside also gives increased power and effect to the bully's attack. It's like buying a T.V set and handing over double the cash. You're allowing the bully to not only hurt your body on the outside but on the inside too. Welcome to self-bullying, great for the bully, and extremely bad for you. The victim is then left with is the combined anger of two people sloshing about inside them like ten pints of lager and a curry.

Anger is a toxic emotion. It makes the victim feel emotionally numb, unable to communicate properly with people and unable to enjoy the times they should be enjoying because their energy is burnt away by feelings of fear and sadness. I'm sure a lot of people who knew me in my teens thought of me as moody and often angry looking. I have since learned to not bully myself and if you want to increase your confidence you need to do the same. Everyone makes mistakes; everyone feels they've let themselves down at some point. The trick is not to beat yourself up about it; it's only through experience and from making mistakes that you learn how to do things right. I love making mistakes because each time it happens I have a good laugh at myself first and then I learn from it. Don't put yourself down ever, when you make a mess of things have a laugh and a joke about it and learn a lesson.

The book you are reading is not at all about being a perfect person and not making mistakes in life. This author has made loads and I'm sure you have too. But rather this book is about learning from mistakes, growing as a person and learning to free yourself from anger and stress in order to live a happier life.

Bullying can have a devastating effect on your life without doubt. There's no fun in being anxious just going to school, or in dreading certain lessons because of who you know will be there waiting for you. It's hard to enjoy life when going to school makes you perspire a lot, have sweaty palms and your nerves feel on edge all the time. Being constantly anxious during the day waiting for the next attack is no way to live your life. You spend thirty plus hours a week at school. If you're a victim that's thirty hours a week of nervous anticipation and fear. It's this kind of extreme pressure that sadly does lead some victims to commit suicide.

Bullying effects every area of your life, unchecked it eats away at your self-esteem and confidence. I myself became withdrawn, moody, shy and as I said full to the brim with anger. My previously high confidence with girls seemed to be on the wane like Shakespeare's moon. At an age when hormones raced around my body like Formula One cars it was extremely frustrating. There were a lot of times I would go out with my friends and end up going home early, angry and frustrated because I was shy and didn't know what to say to people. Some people, meeting me for the first time, would comment on how quiet I was and this would only make me angrier.

Often I would visualize myself exacting violent

revenge on my tormentors. What I didn't realise was that your mind doesn't know the difference between a situation that is real or imagined. When you imagine fighting people your mind thinks you are actually doing it. Your body releases adrenaline, which is not used up because the situation is not real. The extra doses of anger and adrenaline I experienced through these visualizations did nothing to help. The adrenaline you have needs to be released physically (I recommend you get yourself a punchbag) or it simply makes you feel ill. So these visualisations gave me unreleased anger and left me floundering in the quicksand of depression. My own mind bullied me too and often seemed to take sadistic pleasure in telling me how weak I was. By allowing these thoughts to go unchallenged I began to believe that there was no escape from the torment.

Another by-product of being bullied is what I call the 'I'll Show You Mentality'. I found myself doing things to prove to others that I was good. Often that would be to the detriment of actually enjoying my achievements because I would get to one goal and move straight onto the next. The 'I'll show you mentality' was my way of getting back at the bullies, without actually reporting them or fighting them. I'm no Rab. C. Nesbitt but '*I will tell you this*': do things for yourself and enjoy all your achievements, large and small.

Depression

Depression is also a common part of bullying, particularly if you've been a victim for an extended period of time. Student Services fact sheets at *Leeds Metropolitan University* distinguish that a depressed person as suffering from any of the following:

Feelings of guilt or worthlessness,
Loss of concentration,
Suicidal thoughts or planning a suicide
Loss of appetite/energy and weight,
Insomnia or excess sleeping.
Loss of interest in favourite activities
Feelings of hopelessness
Harsh self-criticism

The fact sheets also report that depression has a tendency to make people feel 'numb, empty and despondent'. In terms of bullying I believe depression is caused by bottled up anger, a feeling of being alone with the problem and a sense of shame at allowing yourself to be bullied. Depression always slows you down to the point of in-action where you don't feel like doing anything. Having been an expert in the past at feeling sorry for myself I know for certain that depression = inaction for which action is the antidote.

A victim's sense of shame and adherence to the 'Secret Society' rules of bullying play a big part in worsening the depression. Not telling anyone about your predicament for fear of them thinking less of you is a hurdle the victim must get over. I have to admit to being worried about showing my mates this book and I was very surprised when they read it and did not think less of me for it. In fact one friend told me he thought more of me for having the courage to admit my experiences.

Looking back now at my own experiences of bullying and depression I can see how unnecessary it all was. It all happened because I had no confidence in my ability to fight. If you do not start now and increase your confidence you will assuredly regret it in years to come. You'll probably ask yourself why you were so afraid of a punch in the eye or a few bruises. If this is all that's holding you back at present please consider that in five or ten years time a few bruises or black eyes will be of no importance whatsoever. It's the psychological scars of prolonged bullying that take years to heal.

What I guarantee will be of importance is the confidence that comes from knowing you are able to defend yourself if necessary. The confidence that will come from training yourself to control your thoughts and get yourself to do whatever you have to in spite of feeling fear. This confidence will make you a much less likely target for bullies. The last few years have given me the solutions to my former problems and I'm going to give this knowledge to you. So once you understand it please use it. Have the courage to be honest with yourself about what's stopping you from letting all this anger out and ending your misery.

When you understand what it is that's stopping you making a change you'll be ready to confront it. Whatever solution you choose to deal with the bullies it will involve a confrontation of some kind. The term 'confrontation' is defined by Webster's World Dictionary as 'to face or oppose boldly, defiantly or antagonistically.'

The thing that prevents a victim confronting the problem of bullying is fear, fear of a certain consequence or the 'what if' scenario. However as Rudyard Kipling proclaimed 'Of all the liars in the world, sometimes the worst are your own fears'. If you watch the film 'Rocky III' you can see a great example of defiant confrontation. When Rocky loses his Heavyweight Title to Clubber Lang he is totally beset by fear. He arranges a re-match and goes back into training rather half-heartedly. He confesses to his wife that he is scared and doesn't believe he can win. But once he has admitted his fear he is able to train his hardest and try his very best to win. He accepts that the worst thing that can happen is that he may lose and goes for it.

During the fight he again takes some heavy punches, but instead of cowering he gets more aggressive and antagonises his opponent. In confronting his fear he realises that it is nowhere near as bad as he imagined it to be and he regains the title.

The 'What If' Scenario

Rob was sitting quietly, waiting for the teacher to arrive and the class to start. Suddenly he was slapped very hard across the shoulders by the class bully. He felt his anger rise and began to rise out of his seat, his right hand bunched into a fist.

'What are you going to do about that then?' the bully asked.

Rob thought for what felt like a lifetime, 'Nothing' came his meek reply. Rob sat down. He felt ashamed and weak, sitting in quiet defeat. His fear had beaten him again.

The 'what if' scenario stops most victims from taking action against bullies. My own 'what if' was 'What if I hit him and it doesn't hurt him as I intend?' Here are some other possible 'what ifs' and my suggested replies.

1. What if I tell a teacher and I get laughed at or they tell me it's all my fault?

Answer: Ensure you speak to a trusted teacher who you are on good terms with and who knows you well. Don't give up if the first one does nothing. Go straight to the Head of School if necessary. Remember above all that you are not at fault: the bully is the problem, not you. After all you don't spend your time trying to make someone's life a misery do you? Bullying is a serious issue and a school should take any reports of bullying very seriously. Schools that do not do this are likely in future to be accused of negligence and taken to court by victims.

2. What if I report the bully and they attack me as a result?

Answer: First of all do not let this deter you from reporting the bully. Remember that you have a responsibility to yourself and to every other victim of bullying, to play your part in bringing the bullies out into the open. Secondly take my advice in the chapter 'How to Leave the Victim State and Gain Confidence' and learn to defend yourself. Once you have gained confidence in defending yourself you'll be a lot less worried about being attacked.

Finally I believe that you should turn the 'What if' scenario on its head and use it your advantage. Don't imagine negative happenings e.g. getting into trouble, getting beaten up or laughed at. Instead think of this incredibly motivating 'what if', 'what if' I do absolutely nothing to stop the bullying and I go through years of unhappiness. In my opinion this is the worst 'What if,' are you really prepared to let a bully destroy your life? Or are you going to do something right now to stop them?

Many people who haven't been bullied may look on you as a wimp and tell you 'Oh just hit them back and they'll leave you alone.' I think you'll agree that this is no help at all in terms of advice because when someone has been bullying you they've been holding you in the grip of fear. And when you've experienced a pattern of abuse, the prospect of standing up to the bullying is incredibly frightening. In fact that's why you've been targeted in the first place. I understand how hard it is because it's something I didn't manage to do really because my confidence wasn't there at the time. But you can do it if you build your confidence up high enough. By practising the suggestions I give later for mental and physical training you will become a lot more confident. The quality you need to develop above all though is...

A Sense of Urgency

The idea of becoming confident, successfully ending the bullying and living a happy life must be incredibly exciting for you. It must be so important to you that you'll do everything you can to make it a reality. When I first had the idea of writing this book to help you I was so motivated I stayed up all night with no sleep and wrote until I couldn't write anymore. Similarly the Ali-Wepner fight in 1975 created such a sense of urgency for Sly Stallone that he went home and wrote Rocky, the film that made his name, in three days.

This book will, I hope, motivate you and give you the sense of urgency you need to stop the bullying and start living a happy life again. Nobody can talk from a podium and claim to be fearless because no one is. A few short years ago I was a victim too, I was scared by the bullies. But it's alright to be scared because its just energy you can use to achieve your goals. I made the decision that my life could be far more enjoyable and greater than it was and since then I have been working everyday on overcoming fear. It's an ongoing thing for everyone and every brave person who confronts their fears, however big or small they are grows in confidence.

The main thing is to have that sense of urgency and need to confront your fear and by doing so you will take away the power of the bullies to hurt you. Please don't follow the path of hiding behind anger, alcohol or drugs because none of these things will help you. Facing up to life's little problems is the hardest route but also the quickest way to happiness because you get the confrontation over with. Doing it this way will be hard but there is a helpful Chinese proverb that goes like this 'After the rainfall everything grows.' When the confrontation is over your confidence will have grown and soon you'll be doing the things you've only previously dreamed of in life.

Chapter 7

How To Leave The 'Victim State' And Gain Confidence – Part One

Let me ask you a question; who can bully you? The answer is simply that there is no person or situation in this world capable of bullying you. Only your own mind is capable of doing that. It's your own mind that allows negative thoughts to go unchallenged; it's your own mind that tells you not to fight back when you're attacked because 'you're a wimp'. It's your own mind therefore that has the potential to change your situation. When you accept this you'll start to feel stronger and a smile will break out onto your face.

Once you accept this and begin to train your mind, life gets happier and more exciting. By changing your negative thoughts you take away the power of your mind to bully you. Suddenly you don't need to worry about other people's behaviour towards you. All you need concern yourself with is your reaction to it and your perception of what it means. You should aim to outgrow the bullies and become so strong and confident that you look at their attempts to hurt you with pity. Look at it as a process, life itself is a process. Leaving the victim state will be a process too. Some day's people might succeed in getting you down, don't worry about it, keep trying to get stronger. In time you will look back at yourself and find it unbelievable that you were ever bullied. That's the way it turned out for me. I can no longer identify with the unhappy, bullied teenage that was me because I have grown so much.

It seems to me that there are three worlds we live in. There is the inner world of our minds; the immediate world created by our environment and influences (i.e. your family, friends, school, place of work). Thirdly, there is the external world as a whole. With regard to bullying I often looked at the immediate and external worlds as the source of my problems. I didn't realise that I could resolve it all by making myself happy and strong in my own inner world, my mind. There have always been bullies in people's immediate environments and in the external world. But the true source of the bullying was in my own inner world. It was my mind that allowed my fears and anxieties to eat away at my confidence with each negative thought.

When I first began to change my thinking, life became amazing. I was also shocked that my mind tried to make me hold onto the negative thoughts, making all that darkness and depression seem comforting. I found my thoughts turning to guilt at my new happiness. But I subsequently learned that this is normal when you start to train your thoughts and drag yourself out of depression. To find a way out you've got to keep going forward towards happier thoughts and not look back.

With regards to bullying I sometimes feel that many people don't understand what the fuss is about. Why not just acquire the necessary confidence, confront the bully and nip it in the bud right from the start? And if you wanted it to be I feel it could be that simple. The serious problems come when you've experienced a consistent pattern of abuse over a long period of time. After all what is a fireman's aim with a fire? To put it out straight away before it spreads and does a lot of damage, possibly even killing someone. It's a lot more difficult to extinguish a fire that's been raging for a while. Bullying is like a fire; it usually starts small, like the spark of a lighter but left alone will grow into a towering inferno that dominates everything around.

The longer bullying goes on the harder it is to stop because it becomes normal to the victim. It becomes as normal as a singing live to a sell-out crowd is to Liam Gallagher. You go to school expecting bullying and allow the pattern to continue. It becomes a very big thing to you because in a way it becomes your whole life. Bullying can and does dominate your life, your thoughts, feelings and actions. Consequently it can severely impact on your relations with other people.

Choice

The pattern of being bullied and the role you play as a victim limits you and holds you back from the life you want to live. But did you ever stop and think you have a choice in the matter? I'd have to say 'no' because I myself was blind to the fact that I had a choice. There is choice in every single decision we make in life. You have a choice as to whether you stay in a low paid job or whether you go for something you really want to do. You have a choice of the university you want to apply to, the football team you support. You have choice regarding who your friends are or the music you listen to. We all have choice in everything, but as a victim you don't exercise choice in the way it is meant to be used. At present you have chosen to stay a victim and accept whatever life and the bullies throw at you. A victim is a helpless passenger in a fast car, when they should be the driver going exactly where they want to go and at the speed they choose.

A theme of the film 'Trainspotting' is 'Choose life'

and I think that's a great start. But I say take that further. 'Choose YOUR life and always make the best choice you can.' Don't settle for a life run by some idiot who gives you the 'choice' of the stinging nettles or a good kicking. 'It's your life' and like the fit girl on skates in the early 90s tampon advert, you should choose well.

With bullying or indeed any problem you can either confront it or allow it to kill you or a part of you. A bully's insulting comments are the stimulus that attack you and create a chain reaction effect. An untrained mind will respond to these comments by considering whether they may be true. Even pausing to consider this is a mistake that creates a chain reaction, like a bomb going off that sends negative thoughts all over the place. At this stage it takes a lot of mental effort to fight back so it's better to learn to defeat them right at the start.

Leaving them unchallenged will eventually lead you to depression, the nearest thing to emotional death. Technically you're alive but your mind and emotions have been numbed to the point where you may as well be dead. It's like the stimulus of a hot stove; you either take your hand away or you get burned.

The way to solve your bullying-induced depression in my opinion is to take positive action rather than sit and do nothing. The way back is through being honest about how you feel, seeking help from parents or friends and then to make the changes that will stop the bullying. By confronting the feelings of depression you will fight your way out of it, I know this to be true because I've been there and done it.

So in addition to the physical training you must do to acquire confidence, you must begin right now to train your thoughts. Perhaps I could draw you an analogy to help you understand how you change your negative thoughts to positives. Imagine you're a goalkeeper in the Premier

League, you play for Arsenal and you've got a ponytail. OK, so you're David Seaman. When a shot is struck on goal he does his utmost to keep the ball out of the net, doesn't he?

Now picture the negative thoughts as footballs. You're the goalkeeper (without the ponytail if you wish) and the responsibility is ultimately yours to keep the ball out of the net. What you are doing with your negative thoughts is catching a ball with a frowning, unhappy face drawn on it and changing it to a brighter coloured ball with a happy, smiling face on it.

Here's another analogy.

The Newspaper Editor

When some insecure idiot is sniping at you in class use the red traffic light idea and stop any negative thoughts in your head. You are now in effect a newspaper editor. The newspaper that you edit is your mind. The words in the paper are your thoughts. The idiot is a freelance journalist supplying you with stories. The final decision about which stories go in your paper is down to you. You get to rewrite the stories or comments you are supplied with. If the 'headlines' are negative you can change them to a positive.

As I mentioned earlier if the bully attacks you verbally firstly, go to red on the traffic lights system and reject his negative opinion in your mind, don't allow it any space at all. Then you can go to amber and respond verbally if you wish. Then if he goes to attack you physically you're ready to go to green and defend yourself.

This thought stopping process of going to red should become instantaneous with regular practice. So as soon as the comment is made you must immediately reject it. You can even anticipate it if you see the bully coming. You can say to yourself 'He's going to insult me. Whatever he might say is bollocks and I'm not going to listen to it.' Be ruthless with any garbage thoughts the bully tries to place in your mind. Recognize his or her comments as the great steaming pile of horse manure they are and don't listen to them.

Imagery Techniques

After a tough day at school, I would sit down and replay the days insults in my mind over and over again. An excellent technique is to imagine the bully's comments written on a piece of paper. See them covered in red crosses like a teachers marking and then see yourself setting the paper on fire and smiling as it burns to a crisp. Alternatively you could picture the words or negative thoughts inside a cardboard box and then see yourself stamping all over it until it disintegrates. If the comments produce negative thoughts in your mind you could also picture them as weeds. See yourself ripping the weeds out of the soil with ease and the replacing them with a rose.

This is an internal battle inside your head and it's absolutely vital to your level of happiness. Think of this struggle as similar to the Battle of Britain in World War Two. The invading German Luftwaffe represents your negative thoughts. When the thoughts invade your mind imagine them being sent away by the positive thoughts represented by the RAF.

Self-talk Techniques

If your mind is wandering, and a comment creates a negative thought, then catch the thought straight away. In your head picture it as a burglar with a black and white outfit and a swag bag creeping around your living room.

Turn the light on in the room and watch the burglar bathed in light: he and the negative thought have been spotted. Your thoughts have a voice; they are read to you like a play in your mind. If you notice them as negative then stop the voice, cut it off mid-sentence and don't allow any more to be read. Or similarly you can shout 'stop' in your head when the negative thoughts come in.

A bully's intimidating presence in my experience produces negative thoughts like 'I'm much stronger than you, you should feel terror and sadness now I'm here.' In response to this the victim will cower and agree with this one-sided view. The bully is a weak person wearing a mask of aggression seeking a quick fix for their own insecurity.

Consider that whether the bullies are at school or at work. You may be spending close to forty hours a week in the same environment as these people. So you need to work hard to make that environment a happy one.

All of these mental techniques are based on a simple principle that leads to progress. That principle is…

The Overload Principle

This principle is commonly applied to build muscular strength through weight training. The idea is to gradually increase the weight you use on an exercise. This overloads your muscles and after a period of rest they grow stronger in order to deal more easily with the stress next time. You must also apply this principle to the building of a strong mind. It will be a gradual process but determined, regular practice will bring results.

If you are currently controlled by negative thoughts and you have a great number of them it would be hard to suddenly fight them all. To begin with some will beat your defences. But by practising everyday and constantly trying to increase the number of negative thoughts you turn positive each day you will strengthen your mental defences. In time your defences will become so strong that it won't be such hard work and you'll laugh at the negatives that try to latch onto you and drag you down.

You should also apply Winston Churchill's famous quote to your mental training. 'We will fight them on the beaches, we will fight them on the…' You must commit to fighting these negative thoughts at any time, wherever you are or whoever you're with. If you're going to a job interview and suddenly your thoughts try to focus on your weaknesses; then you need to stop them and focus on your strengths. If you're going to meet a girl or lad for a night out and your mind starts trying to tell you how worthless and ugly you are; then you need to cut those thoughts off straight away. You need to realise that these thoughts are just another chance to get a little stronger and happier. So smile when they come in and focus on everything positive about yourself.

The strength and confidence you need to lose bullying from your life will be acquired by battling with your thoughts inside your own mind. The weaknesses and lack of confidence that allow you to be targeted by bullies find their root in your mind. The bully's behaviour is an external pressure and something you don't control. But by having control of your thoughts and high self-esteem, you can take confident and positive action with the external pressure. Winning this battle inside your head allows you to deal with anything that happens on the outside.

You should now understand the need for physical and mental training techniques. Practise everyday and make it the most important thing you do everyday until you get the confidence you need. You need to feel a sense of urgency; you need to understand that this is your whole life and your happiness at stake. You must be positive and fight back.

Your reaction at all times to a bully should be defence, you must never submit mentally or physically to their attacks. You defend yourself by attacking their comments and any resulting negative thoughts with your mind. Also be ready to exercise your right to self defence if a bully attacks you. Whatever the bully does you launch an attack of your own in response.

Keeping A Record Of Your Progress

Making any big change in life takes a lot of determination and going from being bullied to being happy is no different. Therefore it will help you enormously if you keep a written record of your progress. I suggest you write down details about every incidence of you being bullied and why it happened. When you begin to fight back you should also keep a record of times you have changed negative thoughts for positive ones. Note down times you have used the traffic lights system and reacted positively rather than passively to a bully. To begin with there may be times when you slip up and let some thoughts or actions go unchallenged. It's important to note these too so you can inspire yourself to greater efforts next time.

Keeping a diary may also be very useful if you are asked to provide proof of bullying incidents. Perhaps you could write a diary on a weekly or fortnightly basis. Write down the who, what, where and when of every incidence of you being bullied. At the end of that week or two weeks put the diary in an envelope and send it to yourself by recorded post. When it arrives keep it safe and unopened, the postmark on it will reveal the time period during which you were bullied and may be proof that you are not just making it all up.

Remember that stopping the bullying in your life

should be the most important thing in your life and all your energy should go into it. When your life starts to improve you will laugh at the things that used to scare you (honestly, you will). It will be a huge change that will amaze you when you look back and see how far you've come. So you will never regret putting all your energy into making these changes.

Inspiration

It will also help you to read the books I have listed at the end because these are all people who have overcome what they saw their limitations and the end result is very inspiring. It's also a great idea to write down any inspiring quotes you find through books or films. Write them down and pin them on the wall of your room where you can see them. Then every day you've got a friend telling you how great you are and that it is possible to do the things you want to do. You've got a friend telling you that you can acquire the confidence and skills you desire if you are totally committed and willing to work hard.

So training your mind and regaining confidence is about being assertive with your negative thoughts and every negative influence in your life. Now I'd like to look at a more general philosophy of change.

Building Self-Esteem

Self-esteem is simply the level of regard you have for yourself. I like to think of self-esteem as a muscle. Every one of us has six hundred odd muscles. When muscles are not given regular resistance to contract against they lose their strength.

Every time you've been bullied and have done nothing about it your self-esteem muscle has lost a little of its strength. My self-esteem prior to bullying was comparable in size to one of Sir Richard Branson's balloons. But every incident of bullying squeezed a little more air out until my self-esteem was the size of a shrivelled party balloon that had been left near a hot radiator. Unchecked bullying can shrink your self-esteem radically. You can go from Mr Universe to Mr Puniverse in no time at all.

Bullying did destroy my self esteem, its effect on me was more devastating than Maradona's handball in the 1986 World Cup. It has taken a lot of work since to rebuild it. Bullying gave me a lot of anger and fear, which hampered my relationships with people. I became afraid of speaking to people I didn't know and would often feel very uncomfortable. People would anger me when they said, '*You're quiet aren't you?*'

So how do you rebuild your self-esteem? Basically you achieve this by doing some task, however small each day to build it back up again. You rebuild your confidence and surprise yourself with the things you are able to do.

The most effective way I have found to do this is to take responsibility for doing things that you normally leave to others. Anything you normally give up on for fear of not being able to do it will build your self-esteem. At school, for example, you may normally let other people do the talking in class because bullying has made you quiet and withdrawn. The way to rebuild your confidence is by speaking up. Do it gradually, perhaps aim to make one comment in the first class and as your confidence grows you'll want to speak more and more. Whenever you are confronted by something you have never done before, your mind throws negatives at you and tried to hold you back. It'll tell you it's not worth it, that you shouldn't bother trying. Pushing through this mental barrier and deciding to figure it out, (even if it takes ages) will build your confidence. When I dropped out of the first University I went too, I was determined to re-apply. I went to the local career service and talked to the resident 'expert' about which Uni's to apply too. I had my heart set on going to one particular University city, but he told me my A level grades were too low to get in. so I told him I'd retake my A level if that's what it took to go where I wanted. The 'genius' shifted in his chair a little at my suggestion, looked over the top of his glasses at me and told me that statistics showed that candidates almost never improved their A level grades second time around. He suggested I should settle for a small college in a small town like the one I'd just left. If I had listened to this man he could have crushed my dream flat as a pancake. Just for the record, I did retake my A levels and I did improve my grades and I did go to the University I dreamed of going to and I had an amazing time. Don't listen to people who tell you your dreams are unlikely or impossible. Building self-esteem and achieving what you want in life, is very often about trying your best to do things you're not sure you can do and surprising yourself.

Overcoming my fear of people played a huge part in re-building my self-esteem. I made the decision to stop avoiding social situations and would force myself to open up and talk to people. A few years ago I also got a job as a customer service rep in a busy call centre. This involved me talking to people on the phone 8 hours a day, 40 hours a week. We did two days of training and even role plays and talking aloud in front of ten strangers terrified me. I remember stuttering, my heart racing and my voice quivering. When the time came to go on the phones alone I deliberately held back so I could avoid confronting my fear a while longer.

But after the second day I started to enjoy it and extend my conversations. I had thousands of phone calls and got to speak to people of various ages, including a lot of girls my age. My confidence received a huge boost when I realized I was good at getting on with people. I had one memorable conversation with a girl for over an hour at the end of one day. I realized that she had been interested in me and that I'd made her laugh. And from then on I've chipped away at the fear of people that bullying gave me.

Most recently I've been having singing lessons. Now I'm making progress in something I've never done before. Now I've got the confidence to sing in front of people, I'm certainly not bothered about talking aloud in front of them. In my former job as a fitness instructor I also volunteered to give a seminar presentation on weight loss. Although I was nervous I gave a great presentation and built up my self-esteem a little more.

Sports

Weight Training: For me, weight training played a big part in rebuilding my confidence. I started weight training aged thirteen and played around with weights until I was sixteen when I started to take it more seriously. The gym I trained in had a rack of barbells by the wall from 15kg to 75kg and over about 18 months, I went from being able to bench press the lightest barbell to the heaviest one. This progression was very inspiring to me and it greatly increased my confidence to see my body image becoming more pleasing to me.

If you decide to start weight training, please make sure you get a qualified instructor to show you how to do the exercises properly and to give you a programme to follow. Make the program gradually harder as your fitness improves. Always use proper technique on each exercise because not only will that keep you injury free, it will also make your muscles grow faster. It's also a great idea to train with a friend of similar age and strength so that you can encourage each other. I trained with my best mate at the time and he helped push me further than I could have got on my own. I felt great every time I got a bit stronger, was able to train harder, lift a bit more weight etc. in fact, I deliberately set myself goals in my fitness training that are designed to build my confidence. I've done things that I knew would push me very hard, things like going out running at 6 am and sprinting 10 times up a steep hill with wrist weights on. At that time in the morning, my body just wants to be in bed and my mind always tries to tell me that I can't do it, or shouldn't be up at that time (maybe it has a point!). But I do it anyway. Sports in my view are also good medicine for flagging self-esteem. Sports were in all honesty the reason I actually went to school (and the girls of course). Sport seems to have taken a back seat in schools now, which is sad. Many people seem to have developed negative attitudes towards sport, perhaps because of being forced to do it at school or because they were bullied by those more capable. However there is an enjoyable activity out there for everyone to be involved.

Sports give you increased mental and physical fitness. They teach you to work individually and as part of a team. Sports teach you courage, determination, co-ordination, awareness of others, quick thinking and problem solving. If you've ever played rugby and found yourself at the bottom of a ruck you'll have learnt all about crisis management!

Sports teach you many skills that employers want to check you possess at job interviews. Sports should be a part of everyone's life, in my opinion. They certainly work with regards boosting a person's self-esteem.

The way to succeed is to resolve to follow the task to a conclusion irrespective of how many thoughts tell you to quit.

It's these little victories over yourself that lay the foundations for high self-esteem. Don't allow yourself to shrink in self-doubt in the face of difficult tasks. Rebuild your self-esteem like you were building a wall. Brick by brick.

Chapter 8

How To Leave The Victim State And Gain Confidence – Part Two

Giving over your power to the bully is like being on a see-saw with the power heavy bully on the ground and you up in the air. If the bully jumps off he can send you crashing to the ground at any time. However by undertaking the physical and mental training I am about to describe you can change places with the bully on the see-saw.

Seeking Approval – 'The person who seeks all their applause from outside has their happiness in another's keeping.'

(Claudius Claudianus)

One of the ways victims give away their power is by their need for other people's approval. The society we inhabit seems geared towards seeking the approval of others. What do football players do when they score a goal? They run straight to the crowd seeking their approval and praise. So much in society seems to be about image.

Our society places a great deal of emphasis on 'success' and 'failure' and in particular on the trappings of success. I think it all has relevance to the problem of bullying. Success for me is a certain point off view; a person might see themselves as having succeeded while others might see them as a failure. And what is failure? Failure is again, a judgement or certain point of view.

Society has its own rules on success and failure that are seemingly based around money and image.

People are just people, and whether you have succeeded or failed in life is entirely up to your own judgement. You could be a businessman who loses a fortune and be seen by everyone around you to have failed. But the businessman might see himself as a success because of the personal obstacles he overcame to try his best at the business in the first place. So how (if I can just get down off my soapbox) does this fit in with bullying?

Well, I think that in schools, just as in society, everyone wants to be seen as a success. Everyone wants to be seen with the 'right' people. At school when you're growing up and developing your identity, you can often feel insecure and lack confidence. This is part of the bullying problem as I think many bullies are seen as popular and confident and attract admiring hangers-on like bees to honey. The 'right' people are not seen to be victims of bullies, and that is why I believe you hear so many stories of bullied kids feeling lonely and isolated. I'd like to link the point about success and failure with the idea of perception and reality. I've often found a gap between my own perception and reality. Problems can increase for you with bullying if you start accepting the bully's perception of you as reality.

So what happens when you're being bullied and you don't feel good about yourself? In my experience victims often try to gain the approval of those who are bullying them. They don't feel too good about themselves anyway and when some idiot makes them feel worse the victim is devastated. They often spend time trying to say to the bully 'Well actually I'm all right really, aren't I?'

Often we search for approval in other things too. As a victim and lacking in confidence I would often ask people things like 'Can I really do this?' Or 'Do people like me?'

I'm sure I also drove my mates crazy between the ages of thirteen to sixteen over different girls I wanted to go out with. I'd ask for their approval and assurance: 'Does so and so like me?' 'Do you reckon she'd go out with me?' Then they'd find out that yes they would and I still couldn't find the nerve to ask them!

So my advice is this: if there's a girl or lad you want to ask out, or a sport or anything (that doesn't harm yourself or others) you want to try, then do it. Don't waste time seeking the approval of others. I've learnt that you don't need anyone to tell you that you can do something. By trying and practising you'll soon find out that you can.

As a victim your own fear and insecurity about yourself will be used against you. It's when you stop and think for a split second that the bullies may be right that you're in trouble. When you start thinking 'Maybe I am ugly' or 'maybe my clothes are crap' you're at the start of a slippery slope towards unhappiness. Seeking approval, fear and insecurity grant a bully increased power. I remember riding to my new school on my old BMX bike and being picked on because everyone else had brand new mountain bikes. The next Christmas, my mum and dad bought me a mountain bike and I rode it to school thinking that no one would tease me about it now. Wrong!

Apparently, my new mountain bike still wasn't acceptable because it wasn't a good enough make. I'd advise you right now to stop looking for anyone else's approval because a bully who senses this will never grant you it.

It is difficult when you're growing up but you've got to work at letting go of this need for other people's approval. By building your self-esteem you should learn not to care what people think of you because you know you're all right. I think it's pointless trying to get on the right side of a bully. When they say to you 'You're a w*****r because blah, blah' speak up (and with a smile on your face) say 'Am I really, well, thanks very much' and walk away. Don't get drawn into their game and don't waste anytime pondering anything they say.

The next thing to do though is to address the victim state. A victim stands out like a smile on EastEnders to a bully because of the way victims communicate. As humans we communicate by sounds, words and body language. Amazingly it is not our words or sounds that have the biggest impact upon that communication. It is in fact our body language. This is responsible for sixty per cent of our communication, with sounds at thirty per cent and words at ten per cent.

The victim therefore communicates to the bully that he is a target mainly with body language. By walking with his eyes trained on the floor, by not making eye contact with people or by standing with shoulders slumped forward.

So the first thing to do is alter this body language and take away sixty per cent of the cause of your problems (a pretty big slice, I think you'll agree). From now on, walk confidently with your chin up and your shoulders back, stand tall and look confident and secure in yourself even if you don't feel it. This is achievable; as shown by the recent documentary series 'Faking It'. In one programme a twenty-year-old university student (who had never been to London before or anywhere further than his family's farm) was trained to be a doorman in the East End of London. By altering his body language and the way he used his voice he was able to successfully work on the front door of a popular nightclub. What's more, the regular doormen did not recognize this lad as the impostor.

So don't be afraid to make eye contact with people as you walk past. Admittedly this will be difficult as many confrontations begin with this eye contact and an aggressive challenge. Shortly I'll go on to the training you can do to help you deal confidently with that aggression.

The next thing to address (and watch out because this may surprise you), are the options you have as a victim. Hopefully you will gain power from the discovery that you do have a choice with regards this destructive relationship.

Firstly you could do nothing. You could sit and hope the problem melts away like a chocolate bar left out in the sun. However after reading this book you should realize that this option is about as useful as one of Baldrick's cunning plans to Edmund Blackadder.

Solving bullying is not as difficult as solving a murder case. Morse and Frost and all the other TV detectives have only clues to go on. You the victim, however, know exactly who has bullied you. You know when, where and what they said or did to you. The victim therefore has all the information necessary to solve the 'case'.

Think back to the analogy I gave in an earlier chapter about preparing for an exam. A victim of bullying experiences a great deal of expectation, namely you know who is likely to bully you and you know where it's likely to happen. An exam will take place on a set day and time. You'll know in advance what subject the questions will be on. You'll also have an expectation of the atmosphere in the exam hall, the pressure you'll be under and the way you're likely to feel.

All this information allows you to prepare for that exam. When it comes to being bullied you probably have certain lessons and people in those lessons that will do it. It may be at lunchtime or at home time when everyone is leaving. Therefore you can prepare yourself for this. When you've done some training and increased your confidence you can walk into that lesson, or lunch hall prepared for someone to bully you. You'll know what's likely to happen and you can do something about it.

The option you choose will also be influenced by the type of bully you are facing. In my opinion there are three types of bullies:

Unintentional bullies

As a victim you can become very sensitive to everything said and begin to take the most innocent comments as criticism. Therefore some people's comments or actions may upset you but the person may not know it. They may have no intent at all to bully you or to cause you pain. In this case I think the solution is simply to tell them that they've upset you and take the situation from their reaction.

Hangers-on

The main bully's hangers-on support his or her actions and follow them like sheep. They know that what they are doing is wrong but their behaviour may be motivated by fear or insecurity. They may support the bully for fear of being singled out themselves. They may be insecure about their own identity or some aspect of themselves and feel safer in a group, which diverts its attention to someone else i.e. you. Whatever their motivation the solution is to report the main bully. Once he or she has been disciplined and made an example of the rest of the group should disperse because they no longer have a leader.

Career Bullies

Career bullies are persistent offenders. The negotiation type approach often will not work with these bullies. They see you as such an appetizing and easy snack for their ego that they absolutely have to bully you. In my view the only thing that works here is to report them to the proper authorities so they can be dealt with.

Here then are my suggested options for stopping the bully.

Tell a Teacher/Parent or Big Brother/Sister/Friends

Choosing this option is extremely brave in itself because a victim can often feel ashamed and not want anyone to know. It is estimated by BBC Online that the vast majority of bullying goes unreported. This is attributed to the victim's shame or fear of worse treatment for involving an outside party.

This is simply another part of the game. It's just another rule invented by the bully; the threat goes something like this: 'You tell anyone about this and you'll get worse treatment.' Now if I did a talk on bullying at a school and I asked all the bullies present to stand up, I bet none of them would. They all act tough in front of their mates and you'd think they would be proud of how 'hard' they are. Yet they want the fact that they bully you kept secret. Why do you think this is?

It's simply because the bullies know that what they're doing is wrong. And if any teachers or parents found out and got involved, they would be disciplined. So if the bully himself or herself knows it's wrong, then it definitely is wrong. And any feelings of shame you have should be cast aside because the treatment you're experiencing is wrong. And you must tell enough people about it until one of them helps you.

In my opinion bullying is a sort of secret society. The bully doesn't want anyone to know for fear of getting into trouble. The bully may also know their behaviour is wrong and fear anyone finding out and labelling them a bully.

Likewise the victim does not want anyone to know because of shame, fear of people thinking less of them, even laughing at them. They may also fear people finding out yet telling them it's their fault and offering no help.

It was my sense of shame that stopped me from telling anyone what I was suffering. Once I remember being in a one-sided fight with a group of older lads. One man came out of his house to ask if I needed any help because I'd been punched a bit. He offered to sort the lads out, but my shame at being unable to defend myself led to me declining his offer. I asked my Dad for help and he told me to 'fight my own battles'. The trouble was I didn't have the courage or skills to do so.

If I had a car that travelled back in time when it reached 88 mph, I'd have told the teachers at school. Then I'd have found someone who could help me build my confidence and courage, so I could fight my own battles. I think that telling the teachers and getting the bullies dealt with would give the victim a vital breathing space. They could have time to develop their confidence and would not allow the bullies to harm them again.

The person you tell may be able to help you stop the situation directly or indirectly and a little support and encouragement would not hurt your cause. After all if your parents have a history of helping you through difficult times it would be wise to tell them. If your parents or guardian are not aware that you are suffering they cannot help you. Your parents or guardian do have a certain amount of power once they are aware that you are being bullied. Once you tell them they can make the school aware. Then they can monitor the school's procedures for dealing with the bullies and ensure that your bad treatment stops.

Parents could also mediate between the bully and the victim. The victim's parents could visit the bully's parents and without accusing anyone, explain that there are problems between the two children. If the bully's parents tell the bully to stay away from the victim and vice versa it may solve the problem. The school could be involved and both children could be warned that they will be in trouble if they're seen together.

By telling someone you are taking responsibility and bringing the situation closer to being resolved. Tell all your friends who is hassling you, ask them to back you up and stand up to the bullies as well. A bully will be deterred if a victim has strong support from their friends. Too often a victim is alone in the situation and the bully is shown no evidence of the victim having any support. When my sister was surrounded by a crowd and punched I gave the bully reliable evidence that she had support and it worked.

My sister's two 'friends' had stood by and watched her get attacked, so when she came home upset I was enraged. I went straight to the park where she'd been hit and luckily the girl was still there. I didn't know who she was exactly so I asked a group of kids if they'd seen what had happened. They pointed her out and I went straight over. My first words were *'Why did you hit my sister Emma?'* She denied it straightaway, *'I never hit anybody,'* she said with a look of shame on her face. She wasn't so loud and aggressive now because she knew my sister had support.

She just looked down at the floor and said nothing, so I left it at that and went home. For the next few days I went to pick my sister up from school to let all the kids know she wasn't alone. I wish I could have done more to help her, but I wasn't as strong then as I am now. But I know that this bully never did bother Emma again, so in some way I did help.

So tell your friends, your siblings, your parents, and your teachers. Tell everyone what's happening to you and tell them who's doing it. Remember it isn't your fault, so don't be ashamed. The bully is the one with the problem. A word of warning though. Bullies are devious. No one wants to be labelled a bully and they'll say anything to avoid it. I remember that the first bully I encountered aged five went home and told his mum that I had been bullying him. His mum rushed to school the next day demanding that I (the one whose life was being made miserable by her son) be dealt with. Fortunately, the teacher correctly did not believe that I was or could be a bully.

If however you go to the teachers for help and are not taken seriously, don't give up. My own sister went to the school headmaster about the daily bullying she experienced and was accused of causing the problems herself! If this does happen to you the best solution is to use a little of your anger and determination. Keep telling people and asking for help until you meet someone who will help you. Don't be discouraged if your brave efforts to solve the situation do at first fall on deaf or ignorant ears.

In later years I did have a situation with a bully that led to me reporting him. I had been working as a temp in an office for a recruitment agency. By nature this type of work is insecure and your employment can be ended without notice. However if you, the employee, wanted to leave you had to give a week's notice.

I wanted to leave my job to go to university, so I gave one week's notice and thought nothing more of it until the agency phoned me. The man on the phone demanded to know why I'd left the job he'd got me. When I told him he lost his temper and started putting me down, calling me this and that (I don't know about you, but I don't like being called 'this and that'!). He then told me he would see to it that I didn't get another job.

I was absolutely livid and had to talk myself out of going straight down to the office to 'see' him. But I realized that if I did that he would be seen as the victim and I would get into a lot of trouble. Instead I got all of my anger out in a letter of complaint. The next day I went to the agency and gave my letter to the manager. I outlined what had happened, what the man had said, how it made me feel and requested that his behaviour be dealt with.

The manager was very apologetic and assured me that he would be spoken too. A few days later I received a letter of apology. The agency told me the man had been disciplined. They also told me that I had been right to speak up about him and wished me all the best at university.

So you can see that reporting bullying, despite your fears, is very effective.

Another solution to bullying is what I call The Mental Defence

When it comes to bullying I've found that it's often your mind that is the bully. Someone might make a comment, for example that you don't like and you might take that comment and use it to beat yourself up. I was guilty of this but now I know better I won't ever beat myself up again. Bullying is no longer a part of my life, but I haven't had to fight any bullies to achieve this. What I have done is strengthened my mind, the high sense of self-worth I now have will not allow me to be bullied. My mind can no longer bully me either because I have trained it to be strong. Often you don't have to stop the bully, you just have to stop bullying yourself and that is enough.

When your mind is weak, bullies are successful in striking a raw nerve with their comments because the victim feels sensitive about some aspect of themselves. By not being concerned by anyone else's opinion you take away most of the power of these comments to harm you.

From this point on the comments are merely an unfortunate reflection of someone else's insecurities.

When these comments do hit a raw nerve the victim's head seems to go down and they accept it as the truth. Then the mind takes over and searches for bad times in your life to back up your tormentor's statement. Someone may say for instance: 'You're crap at football, why are you in the team. My mates better than you are... Blah, blah etc.' Suddenly your mind is busy recalling every open goal you've missed or pass you've miskicked.

The solution is simply to use your mind to crush the bully's attack. You could ignore the comment or better still use it to strengthen your mind. For example you can think 'I am good at football, I wouldn't be in the team if I wasn't. I enjoy playing and that's all that matters.'

Another solution may be to desensitize yourself to the verbal abuse. I had to start wearing glasses at the age of five, those attractive NHS black ones too! I lost count of the times I was called 'four-eyes' at school. At first it upset me and then after a while it just made me yawn and say, 'You'll have to do better than that.'

If you decide to do self-defence training you can use verbal abuse in that training so you're not bothered by it. As Dave Turton said to me in the interview for this book, if you're regularly called a 'fat bastard' or 'lanky streak of piss' or if you've got ginger hair and your bullies say 'oi walking match', get your training partners to call you this in practice and very quickly the bully's words will lose the ability to upset you.

Verbal Response

After your mental defence you could use a verbal response to the bully. You could cut to the chase and tell them how little their opinion means to you. Tell them they're wasting their time trying to hurt you because you don't care what they think. It is worthwhile getting a sheet of paper and writing down some confident responses to the bully's comments. Bullies are often like stuck records in that they use the same remarks again and again. Write down their usual comments and prepare a response to each one and then learn it like a script for a play.

One time at school I was made captain of the football team and picked to play out of my normal position in centre midfield. The lad whose place I'd taken came up to me and said 'Why are you playing there. You can't even head the ball.' To be fair he had picked out a weakness of mine but with a prepared comment I could have picked out one of his and said 'Why are you left side of midfield when you've got no left foot, you thick bastard?' However his approach caught me unprepared. Bullying is a game; you have to be prepared when the bully wants to play it with you.

The trouble is that often the bullying comes from totally out of the blue. Someone might insult you and then walk off, leaving you shocked and trying to think of a reply. So the solution is to be prepared with an answer to any approach the bully uses.

The Warning

Give the bully a warning e.g. 'I know what you're trying to do. Stop bullying me or you'll be in a lot of trouble.' And when you give the warning, mean it. The key to success with this is to only give them one warning. If they don't stop you have to report them or they won't take you seriously.

This approach is like the football ref who deals with foul play. Depending on the individual, he might have a word with a player after the first bad tackle. The next time he might give a yellow card and the threat of a sending off if he does it again. If it happens again the ref has to give a red card and send the player off, it's in the rules.

There are rules to the game of bullying but as I said these are established by the bully. So what about establishing your own rules? Set your own rules to what you're prepared to tolerate and follow them to the letter. Perhaps you might let one comment go with a warning. But if it happens again your rules say that you will confront the bully and tell them to treat you with respect or you will report them.

The Challenge

If someone has threatened to harm you physically, you can challenge him or her to try to do that, or you could smile and say, 'No you couldn't' and just walk off. I discovered at school that most of these threats were hot air and would have been more useful to Sir Richard Branson in his next balloon flight. Some people just want to appear hard in front of their peers, some bullies are jealous of you, some just want to be popular and others just want to draw attention to themselves. They only want to see you show fear at their threat. Train yourself to not show any and do not submit to their threats.

The Physical Response

Proper self-defence training will help you overcome your fears and will make you less of a target for bullies. If you will not confront a bully about their behaviour and tell them they're upsetting you because you're afraid they'll beat you up, then self-defence training is the answer.

With increased confidence you'll be able to talk to the bully knowing that if they get aggressive and attack you,

you are easily capable of handling it. When you are really confident, you'll be able to walk away from the bullies, who try to drag you into a confrontation. You'll do this because you know they can't hurt you because you can defend yourself. Please refer to the interviews with Dave Turton and Geoff Thompson for advice on this.

I like to call the physical response: the 'George McFly approach!' In the movie *Back to the Future* George is bullied continuously throughout the film by Biff (the school bully). It's a great example of bullying as Biff has his own gang of sheep-like hangers on who follow his orders. George is shown earlier in the film trying to laugh along with Biff as he taps his head and asks if there's 'anyone home'.

There's a fantastic scene at the end when George is being held in an arm lock by Biff and he gets mad and knocks Biff out. Though he hadn't displayed any aggressive tendencies throughout the film George McFly found that he did have the answer to being bullied all along, he just didn't believe in himself until he got so angry he forgot about his fear. The important thing to grasp is that you can't rely on others to stand up for you. The interview with Emma explains how a gang on the way home encircled her and two 'friends' from school. The gang were urging this one girl to hit Emma, being weak and led by the crowd she did. Emma didn't hit back and her two 'mates' failed to rally round her against the gang. The lesson to learn here is that you can't rely on anyone else to defend you.

These options function in a similar way to a set of traffic lights. When the bully attacks verbally you go to red and reject any negative thoughts in your mind. Then you can go to amber with a verbal response or even a challenge. At this point you should walk away, still keeping your eyes on the bully. And if the bully pursues you, put your arm out to keep them at a safe distance, look them in the eyes and tell them firmly to leave you alone. If the bully tries to attack you, go to green and protect yourself if you need to. This idea will be explained more fully in the mental training section. Firstly I will give you suggestions on how to acquire confidence in physically defending yourself from a bully.

We all know that fighting goes on in schools. We all know that when one starts everyone rushes round to have a look. Fighting is a part of school life; it was a common feature of all the schools I've attended. The fighting I really can't stand is the one-sided fighting of a bully against a victim. That's the fighting that needs to be phased out.

Having been bullied I know that both reporting the bullies and increasing your confidence are vital. In my opinion reporting the bullying will help, but you must increase your confidence because in life you will always meet bullies. If you do nothing to develop your confidence the next bully that comes along will victimize you, continuing the cycle. You must develop your confidence or you will go through life being bullied by anyone who wants too.

Self-Protection Training

I WANT TO MAKE IT CLEAR THAT I AM NOT ADVISING YOU TO TRAIN YOURSELF TO BEAT UP THE BULLY AT SCHOOL TOMORROW. My aim here is to point you in the right direction of people who can help you acquire the necessary physical skills. I don't plan to go into too much detail because there are many people far better qualified than myself to teach you self-protection. What I will say though is that anything you do learn should be very simple and easy to apply if you are forced to defend yourself against a bully. Your goal should be to learn a few simple physical techniques. I understand that not everyone has a background in sports, but learning these physical techniques is easy if you are willing to work hard at them.

You may feel that you couldn't fight or that you are not particularly well co-ordinated. But the acquisition of any skill is simply about focused repetition. By that I mean that you understand what you're doing and why you want to learn it and then you practice over and over until you're good at it. If you feel you can't fight back, don't worry, you can learn. If you want to play the guitar, sing or ride a motorbike, you can learn. And once you are confident in these physical techniques, your days of being bullied should be numbered.

If you haven't seen the movie Rocky V then I recommend it for the example it sets to anyone who wants to stop being bullied. Rocky's son goes to a rough new school and on his first day gets beaten up. The next day he gets beaten up again and robbed of his money.

Rather than allow this to continue he goes to his dad's boxing gym to train. In one of those inspiring music videos (typical of the series) we see him training hard, getting fit and learning to hit hard. Rocky meanwhile is oblivious to his son's problems and offers no help. Enraged at this Rocky Junior takes responsibility for sorting it out himself and channels his anger into training harder.

The next time he is confronted at school the bully threatens to 'pound his teeth out'. Instead of cowering Rocky Junior challenges the bully to make good on his threat and wins the resulting fight. It was an extraordinary transformation from a victim to a strong confident boy. This is the change you too should work hard to make.

Likewise in the movie *The Karate Kid*, Daniel eventually conquers the bullies. However in this instance the situation is slightly different because Daniel is prepared to fight back right from the start. The only problem is that his fighting skills are not comparable to the team of lads who victimize him. So he has to undergo physical training with his mentor until he is skilled enough to defend himself.

A visit to the local ABA boxing gym or a good kickboxing club will help you acquire the necessary techniques to hit hard and defend yourself. I personally recommend you get in touch with either The British Combat Association, The Self Protection Agency (Spa.ukf.net) or Dave Turton's Self-Defence Federation for expert training and a realistic approach to self-defence. You can also read the advice of Dave Turton and other excellent martial artists in the monthly magazine Martial Arts Illustrated. Another excellent source of advice is Alan Charlton's page in Fighter's Magazine.

Putting their advice into practice will give you the confidence you will need if you are forced to defend yourself.

Boxing has been a great experience for me. I was a member of my university club and trained twice a week for two years. Joining a club can give you a sense of belonging and I myself made some fantastic friends in my time there. The training enhanced my physical fitness, and self-esteem, and although hard work it was fun.

Training in boxing is also especially beneficial because it gives you a physical release for all your anger and stress. There's nothing more therapeutic in my opinion than punching a heavy punchbag until you reach exhaustion. Training at a good club or even installing a punchbag in your own home will be a great investment of time for you. It even allows you to practice situations with the punchbag as the bully. You can practise your verbal responses, using your lead hand to keep the bully at a safe distance. And you can draw a bully's face on the bag and practice hitting it, letting out your aggression as you do so.

You can practice these simple techniques that I learnt from Dave Turton, with a friend. One of you should walk towards the other and be very aggressive, use swear words and threats. The person being attacked should put out their left hand (if you punch right handed) and stop the attacker from coming closer than an arms length away. You then tell the attacker firmly and aggressively, speaking from your stomach (not your throat) to get away from you. If the attacker still comes forward you can choose to hit them. It's very simple and each practice session will make you more confident in dealing with bullies.

Punching

Learning good punching technique is simply about repetition. Practice on a punchbag or in front of a mirror. The best punches to learn are the ones that create most impact, e.g. the hook, cross or uppercut. Start from a good stable base and focus on twisting your hips as fast as you can. So if you throw a right hook twist your hips fast to the left creating a space for your arm and shoulder to come through. This puts all of your body weight into the shot.

Sparring

Training in a sport like boxing, wrestling or kickboxing will help you get used to fighting and the emotions that accompany it. It important to begin with light contact so you can gain more confidence in your skills. Then you can gradually increase the intensity of the sparring to full contact (provided you wear a gumshield, sparring gloves and protective headgear of course.) It's important to train with people of different ability levels. If your problem is an inability to raise aggression to deal with bullies then sparring will teach you to develop it because you learn to either fight back or get a beating. Get as much practice as you can and build confidence in yourself. You should aim to emerge from your victim persona like a butterfly from a caterpillar. In the next chapter you will see how I did this myself...

Chapter 9

Understanding My Fear

A great example of the 'bully/victim relationship' can be found in the movie *Gladiator*. Maximus has just become a slave and is waiting to face the gladiators for the first time in the arena. One man at the front of the queue is shaking with adrenaline; he loses control of his bladder and urinates all down his leg. When he is released into the arena he panics, freezing with fear. He is easily killed. Maximus, on the other hand, has experienced many battles and instead of panicking accepts that he has to fight in order to live. He is focused and aggressive and, using his adrenaline to drive him on, he annihilates the gladiators.

In the 'bully/victim relationship' the victim is the slave who panicked with fear. The example you must strive to follow is that of Maximus. He has trained to fight and has much experience of having to fight and of feeling scared. Therefore he is able to take positive action in the face of the gladiators or bullies.

As a victim you are allowing your fears to hold you back from attaining happiness. By training your mind and engaging in physical training you can learn to control your thoughts so they help rather than hinder you. The end result you should be looking for is a combination of mental and physical confidence. You need to be confident that you can defend yourself. You also need to be confident in being able to take a confrontation as far as necessary. If for example, you are able to persuade a bully to leave you alone by talking to him or her that's great. But if the bully wants to fight you need to be confident you can deal with that too.

When I was a victim I was always afraid of being hit. But looking back I can honestly say that although I was punched many times, not one of them actually hurt me. All it did was set my adrenaline off and afterwards I would wonder why I was physically shaking.

My point is therefore that being hit by a bully is nothing to fear. Therefore I think it is an excellent idea to sit down with pen and paper and write down in total honesty exactly what you're afraid of. Why are you allowing people to treat you as though you were worthless? Having established this you can work to remove the fear's power over you.

The way to a solution is having the courage to be honest with yourself. It takes great courage to do this. The man in the pub, for example, who is annoyed after a row with his wife and attacks someone innocent, hasn't got the courage to be honest with himself. It may be helpful to answer these questions:

In what way are you being bullied? What sort of things do people say or do to you?

What emotions do you feel when you see the bully at school?

How do you feel inside when you are being victimised and how do you feel afterwards?

If you feel anger when you are being victimised, what stops you from expressing your anger?

What methods does the bully use to keep you scared?

Do you think the bully knows he or she is causing you pain?

Answering these questions should help you reach a

better understanding of yourself and your situation. It should allow you to see what personal qualities you need to cultivate to solve the problem.

I went from being happy and outgoing to shy and withdrawn. It got to the stage where I would be afraid to speak in front of people in case they didn't like me or what I said.

Over the last two years I have also reached a greater understanding of myself and the reasons I always gave in to verbal intimidation and aggression. My own training and reading the work of people who had acquired the confidence and security I wanted has been a very successful combination.

I increased my self-esteem and confidence by training in boxing in order to learn to hit hard and develop aggression through sparring. The first time I stepped through the ropes to spar with a headguard, gumshield and fists like footballs is an occasion I will never forget. It is obvious to me now that the lads I boxed took it very easy on me (just throwing light jabs). But at the time I couldn't control my breathing and adrenaline, and I was scared sh**less.

However each week I would try again and over time I could cope well with a lot more aggression. Every week I faced a lonely walk to the gym, once there it was a battle just to get in the ring. I would be stood outside the ring thinking 'Rob, you don't need to do this' and 'I hope I don't have to spar against him.' After overcoming this mental battle I would often have no fight left in me when I actually did get in the ring. Sometimes after a few rounds I would give in to my mind and stop when I was tired. But as my confidence grew I began to enjoy the challenge and the psychological high afterwards.

However, boxing, sparring with 14 ounce gloves with no verbal aggression allowed was nothing like the violence you see in the pub and this still scared me.

The next step for me was to break my fear down further in order to establish exactly what I needed to learn. I realised initially that my fear had been based on a lack of confidence in the power of my technique, i.e. I realised that I couldn't punch my way through a soaking wet paper bag that already had a hole in it. However by training in boxing I had improved my technique and power and developed a lot of confidence.

Then I broke my fear down again and realised that it was based on a lack of confidence in dealing with aggression. To accomplish stage two I was advised to seek out Dave Turton of the British Combat Association for a lesson.

Over the course of an hour and a half I learned how to protect myself by defending my personal space assertively against an attacker. I learnt all about verbal and aggressive posturing and how to use a verbal and physical 'fence' in any situation.

What I also discovered was that I didn't need to learn a textbook full of techniques. In fact I came away confident in two specific ones. I realised that if I'd known this years ago the bullies would have been eclipsed without a problem.

What I came away with most of all was a change of attitude. The lesson dragged me from the 'victim state'. It was explained to me that when attacked we all are scared. What you must do is keep your thoughts positive, tell yourself that you're going to beat the attacker. He said you should turn the energy of your adrenaline into anger. Be angry with the person for attacking you, be assertive tell them to keep away. If they still come forward then you have to defend yourself.

I have since employed aggression in my training and am beginning to realise that I have nothing to be worried about. All it required was confidence in a couple of simple techniques and a change of attitude. Instead of my previous thoughts of 'What if I get attacked? I can't handle it!' I began to think more positively. I realised that I would notice most potential situations before they developed. If one did escape my observation and I was attacked, I now had the skills to deal with it.

Honesty and an analysis of my fear allowed me to release the stranglehold it had on me. I did not have a fear of violence or fighting but ultimately a fear of aggression. Having understood this I have reached an all important understanding of myself.

I no longer need to be paranoid about violence or bullies. I have found the vast majority of people to be friendly, non-threatening and great. There are more worthwhile things in life for me or anyone else to be doing other than fighting or being worried about fighting.

In the words of Edmund Blackadder, 'I want to be young and wild, then I want to be middle aged and rich and then I want to be old and annoy people by pretending I'm deaf.' In my life I have decided that a fear of fighting is no longer going to bully me or dominate my thoughts.

Chapter 10

Don't Look Back In Anger

It takes a great deal of work to go through being bullied and to come out the other side. And nobody ever comes away unscathed. There is a way however, to deal quickly with the left-over anger and move on with your life. When you have made the changes I have described you may be tempted by a desire for revenge on those who have hurt you. In my opinion it is not a worthy use of time and as I said earlier we have too little time in life to play any part in the 'bully/victim relationship'. However having gone through bullying and come out the other side you will have emotions of anger and sadness that you need to confront and deal with.

Bullying affects the victim psychologically as I have said. The way to come to terms with these effects after bullying is to represent the experience in a positive way in your mind.

The effects of bullying can haunt you and cast a shadow over your life if you allow it too. I myself experienced several years of frustration and unresolved anger. I resolved it by confronting all the feelings that accompanied the aftermath of bullying.

I believe that alcoholics at the AA stand up and admit to everyone present that they are an alcoholic. This is the first step on the road to recovery. For me personally the first step was getting over the deep sense of shame and admitting it to myself, that I had suffered, felt burning anger, sadness, depression and fear.

When I admitted to myself that my self-esteem had taken a battering I was able to rebuild it again.

Prior to this I just wallowed in my depression and anger. I was 18 years old, two years after the bullying had ended, at a university I didn't like and a town I hated. In going there I hadn't exercised my right to choose. I'd gone because people had told me that 'Any university's better than not going at all.'

My depression became a regular companion and his drinking buddy anger was forever hovering in my doorway on 24-hour call. The thoughts I was thinking at that time were thoughts I had never thought before. I know that I sunk right to the bottom and had never before or since, been so low in my life. Eventually I contracted glandular fever and went home (which frankly came as something of a relief). At home I began to confront my depression and lift myself back up. I returned to university for one week before I made the decision that began my catharsis. I decided that I could do better and that a life of despairing thoughts was not for me.

I packed my stuff and walked out of the door. The comforting arms of depression called out to me with and asked me not to leave. But I walked away and didn't look back. My life has never been the same since. I confronted all my anger and by talking about it, I healed myself.

Once you have done this yourself you need to move on. To my knowledge revenge has not benefitted anyone in the long run. It seems only to produce further conflict. Years ago, for example, Britain and France sought to make Germany pay for the devastation of World War One. This created a simmering resentment lasting for twenty years until Hitler took actions that produced another war of destruction.

When you have become confident and are free of

bullying you will be happy. There is really no need to resolve to hurt those who hurt you. Such courses of action will only delay what is an exciting transition to a better life. Bullying at this stage is a part of your past; so don't get stuck in a time-warp – move on and look back only to find strength in your experience. It's really not necessary to make an 'evil' miniature clone of yourself and try to take over the world! If you have ever seen Star Wars – The Phantom Menace you may perhaps recall Yoda the Jedi master saying 'Fear leads to anger, anger leads to hate and hate leads to SUFFERING.'

Once you are free of the victim state congratulate yourself on what is a great achievement and move onwards bearing no malice to anyone. Make a point of forgiving your tormentors and especially forgive yourself. Do not beat yourself up for being affected by a bully's behavioural problems. As Mr Gallagher of Oasis has said to millions of people worldwide 'Don't look back in anger.'

It is my opinion that in life we do the best with whatever information we have at that time.

As a teenager I did not have the information I needed to turn my life around. But now YOU do and armed with it you must apply it with determination to your life. I sincerely hope I have educated you about bullying and have taken away any excuse or possible reason for you continuing to let anyone and I mean anyone, bully you.

Please don't allow your feelings of anger and shame to continue to bully you years after the event. Neither should you beat yourself up mentally, admit to yourself that you've been bullied but that it's all in the past. You're stronger and more confident now. Be assured that you did the best you could with the capabilities you had at the time. Forgive your bullies. Forgive them because they were far, far weaker than you ever were.

Chapter 11

The Interviews

Dave Turton
Emma Higgs
Nigel White
Dan Newbold
Tim Bartlett
Geoff Thompson
Reuben Cole
Gavin Jasper
Ex-bully (Name with held)

Dave Turton

7th Dan & Senior Instructor To The British Combat Association

What are your thoughts on bullies and victims?

'Bullies and victims are the same. Bullies are victims of themselves. People bully for a reason, not because of peer pressure, but because they've got a reason to do it. A bully is very very good at picking victims subconsciously. If you're going to stroke a dog and you've got a choice of two dogs, you don't choose the one that's snarling. Bullies find people they think will give them what they want; it's a compensation for something that's missing in their lives. The victims have something they can get over. The bullies have only got one answer and that's to keep bullying.'

From a victim's point of view what is the answer to bullying?

'There's two ways to stop a war. One is when one side defeats another and two is if both sides make friends. The solution is not to bribe the bully, say give them 50p a day not to harm them because that's still bullying. Just say to them 'Why are you doing it?' and if he turns round and smacks you, you're no worse off than when you started. Try to establish communication first and foremost and then if that doesn't work the answer is to produce a less victim orientated person. So what you're looking at is someone with a little bit more confidence. What you don't want to do is go running to the teacher. I know they say 'tell us about bullying' but all that's doing is saying again 'I made him frightened enough to go running to the teacher.' Even though he might get a slap for it or get expelled it's still feeding his bullying. What you need to do firstly is to make peace with the guy, find out why he's doing it. Invite him round for a meal, if you've got a Playstation game he hasn't got then offer to swap. You're not bribing him, you're trying to make friends with him.

If you've got to get into the physical side of it then it's difficult. The laws in school are too black and white for me. I disagree with the idea that if you punch him you're as bad as him. If the bullying continued I would be tempted to say there's always a way to do somebody and if the bullying continues, get him back.'

What makes a victim stand out?

'A victim stands out paradoxically because he's not standing out. It's a predatory thing. Lions and tigers have done this for thousands of years, without knowing why they can pick the weakness in the herd. They don't look for the one charging out front they look for the one struggling at the back. If you've got thirty school kids in a yard all talking away they'll be one who won't be joining in as much, who isn't quite as noisy. He tends to want to be in the circle but not so deep that he's noticed. So he stays peripheral on the outside. The guys in the middle of the circle will recognize that he's never in. What he's doing is saying to the bully 'I'm here to be picked on' so it's not a case of him standing out it's a case of him standing in. He's there but not there, he's a non-entity.

If he's stood just listening in, not making contributions the person becomes overt by his covertness.

He's spotted more by what he's not doing and people think 'Oh, he's not going to do anything.' So the bullying will start at a very low level first of all. Things like 'Pass us that ball', and if he does it he gives the bully one point because he's obeyed the command. It's like a game of tennis and the bully has the advantage. So the next time the bully is less polite for example, 'Give us that now'. So he starts giving more and more orders and then he's got him. He's caught him in the trap for as long as the victim isn't giving it back.

In the very early stages, it's too late once it's started, non-compliance or non-aggressive. Non-compliance, for example, saying 'Get it yourself' then walking off is enough. The bully might think 'Right I'll have him next time I see him.' But the bully will have a doubt because the person has done something. There's the analogy of the French priest in World War Two. The Germans said, 'We've taken over here and you will bow down to everything we say, right?' But the priest didn't answer until eighteen months later when the Allies took over the village. Then he walked up to the German commander and said 'The answer is no'. He hadn't complied, he'd done enough to survive. He'd stood up to him in his own little way. You can say no without being too aggressive and I think that's what a victim has got to do.'

Is it the victim's responsibility to sort it out?

'Yes, if a dog's going to bite everybody and you're in control of the dog that's OK. But if it goes out it's the person the dogs going to bite that's got to stop it happening. The victim needs to say to him or herself 'How, without getting my face slapped can I turn around and say no?' Even doing this once will tilt the balance. But usually it's a bit like watching your hair grow. You don't realize you need a haircut till it's too late. You don't realize you're a victim of bullying sometimes until it's too late. You need to nip it in the bud very early!'

When is it too late to stop it easily?

'It's too late when you've obeyed him about half a dozen times because then it can become normal. Physical bullying particularly amongst the younger end usually follows verbal intimidation. That happens for a few weeks first. For example, a bully might say 'Get that ball and bring it over here'. If the person says 'No you get it!' then it may become physical sooner. But you've already stood up to the bully. Once you've gone through a few weeks of being his slave then you can become his physical slave and that's when the physical side starts. So the sooner you stop it the better.'

What training would you do with a 14-year-old kid who's tried mediation and realizes he needs to learn to fight?

'You have to make the training simple and pressurize him at a level that he can take. You do need to get eventually into the physical. Personally the better I got at martial arts the less I wanted to fight anybody. One of my old teachers was once threatened and one of his students said 'Why didn't you hit him?' He replied 'Because I'm a great martial artist and I've saved him from a terrible beating.' What the lad needs to do is develop confidence in his physical ability. Really it's a vicious circle. The guys who are the best at sports are probably picked on the least because they have a natural physical prowess. And if for example a victim did judo for 6 months on the quiet and then it's reported in the paper that he's just won a local competition, you can bet half of the bullies will think 'Bloody hell – he does judo!'

So it comes from feeling confident about yourself in any aspect. It might be that he's got a good singing voice and can sing in the school choir, for example. Learn some very basic self-defence techniques rather than go into the martial arts because every kids into the martial arts now and they're used to seeing Van Damme and the movements of martial arts. Good things to learn are how to use a 'fence', tell the bully to back off and avoid going into dialogue. You don't need dialogue, you just say 'Stay where you are'. Just practise three or four movements and get good at those. It's important to train with someone better than yourself at all times so you realize that you're under pressure in training. Within three to four months good training can turn a victim's life around; that's guaranteed.'

What advice do you have for the victim who knows he needs to throw a punch to defend himself but is held back by fear?

'What you do is train a signal. We do it in running. 'On your marks, set, go.' Some runners go before but very few stay behind. What you've got to do is make a signal in your head, a short word. When you train, that signal starts off a physical flurry. You need a word in your head. It shouldn't be one you use often, but should be your signal to go. In karate kata's they have the *kiahh* in the same place e.g. '1, 2, 3 kiahh' and it's almost the only time they're allowed to shout and punch at the same time. You can stand in front of your punchbag, in your head say a short, strong word and then punch. If you do this in training you can't not do it in reality because that word is the trigger for it. You see it with swimming; they take their marks and await the signal to dive in.

Once you've told the bully to back off you're looking for a signal. That signal is the first forward momentum he makes. Say your word and then hit. Do it in training and you'll do it in reality. It needs to become subconscious as a movement; it needs to become something you recognize. We do it at traffic lights all the time. You sit there waiting for that light to go from red to green. If you don't go on green and there's someone behind you, you think that the other driver is saying 'Get a move on'. You're feeling bad because you've not gone on green. And that same principle will work in your physical.'

Is it fear of verbal intimidation that keeps someone a victim?

'Yes, it's unfamiliarity with something. If you've never handled a snake and think you're afraid of snakes and after a year of being familiar with them you pick it up and throw it away because it's familiar now. Most people are more afraid of consequences than actions, frightened of what's going to come. If you push people physically you've got to push them emotionally as well. You can't really train one without the other. You can lift weights all day but if someone is screaming at you you'll perform differently. Whether it's better or worse you'll perform differently.

You need to act out scenarios, you need people to call you what people will call you on the street, for example, 'You lanky bastard'. If you can't deal with it in training you won't deal with it on the street. Don't be frightened of swearing in training because anything that familiarizes you lessens the shock. The best analogy is the first aid man. He can be on the beach in Ibiza and see someone fall over injured. It's familiar to him and he knows how to deal with it because he's done it so many times before. So in training get people to walk up and push you and see how you feel with it. You have to wind it back to the worst case scenario. In a fight the worst case is that you could die. Anything else is a bonus and to be honest most of them aren't that bad. Once you make people realize that their training is probably harder than a real fight then they'll have legitimate confidence. You must pressurize people physically and emotionally and once its familiar you can deal with it.'

Emma Higgs

Former Target of Bullying

Are there different types of bullying?

Yes, and everyone deals with bullies in a different way. Bullying can be mental, physical and emotional and if you get all three thrown in together it's the worst thing imaginable. Physical is obviously being beaten up. Mental is verbal abuse that gets you thinking that what the bully says is true. And emotional is being taunted and teased in a way that gets you upset.

Do you think both bullies and victims are insecure in some way?

I think that people who bully are often bullied themselves, perhaps by their parents or they're insecure and want to follow the gang. Victims are insecure in a way that people can pick up on it and make them feel even worse about themselves. They can have a go at them and feel great because they can put someone else down. I think bullies will pick on anyone they know they'll get a reaction from.

You can tell a victim from the way they walk, stand and look when people talk to them. But people who've been bullied can become bullies themselves; it's just a big circle.

One girl was picking on me, for example, and she said

something about Mum and I just belted her one and pushed her over a wall. It was bad enough her picking on me, but picking on my family really annoyed me. So I hit her as hard as I could and pushed her over a wall. It was a bit of a turning point for me because she never bothered me again. Then another girl in PE kept slapping me and wouldn't leave me alone. So I told the teacher and he told me to hit her back. He turned his back so I belted her and she never touched me again. But she went crying back to another teacher and I got in trouble for it.

In what way did being bullied change you as person?

When I was younger I was really confident and really popular. But when we moved house and I was being bullied I just didn't like myself and thought there was something wrong with me. It really pushes your confidence down and you start to walk with your head down and eyes looking at the floor.

What was it like going to school every day?

I didn't want to go at all because the teachers wouldn't help me, and even my friends were turning against me.

So you told the teachers?

Yes and the headmaster. The deputy head found out and blamed me for it, so every time they talked to one of the bullies they turned it round and blamed me. It was strange because I couldn't understand why and it made me think that perhaps it was my fault. I thought there might be something wrong with me because people kept picking on me. It took me a few years to re-learn that I was all right but in a way I don't think you ever recover.

So what would you change about your experience if you could go back?

I'd probably beat the crap out of all of them. I definitely wouldn't stand there all scared and take it like I did. I'd stand up for myself and make people listen to me. Whether the teachers listened or not or whether I got into trouble or not I'd still sort them out, because as soon as you hit back they stop it then and they won't touch you.

Was it fear that stopped you from doing it earlier?

Yes, I was scared both of being hurt and of getting into trouble. I could easily sort it out now if any of them tried it again, but when I see them they won't look at me, they just walk past with their heads down. But now I don't care what people think of me. Bullying changes the way you perceive people when you first meet them. You almost expect them not to like you. If they say something just for a joke you think they don't like you and expect them to start picking on you.

Do you think people are more susceptible to being bullied as teenagers are because they want people's approval so much?

Well, I think that bullying can go on throughout your life really; it's whether you let people get away with it or not. It can happen anywhere.

What then is a solution for the victim?

Basically to learn to like themselves. To realise that it

isn't them, there's something wrong with the bullies. There's something wrong with their confidence if they have to pick on people and make them feel small. It's not just the popular people that pick on you either, it's just about anyone because they quickly learn they can get away with it. You must like yourself and just not care what other people think. If someone makes a comment to you in school, just ignore it, walk off, act like it doesn't bother you and never let it show if it does. If you get surrounded by a crowd or whatever then just walk away, don't waste your energy shouting back, just walk off. It's really a case of what you think is possible at the time, whether you're capable of hitting somebody back.

Should fighting be a last resort or could you try to confront the bully and say 'what's your problem?'

You could try that but they usually just give you a load of rubbish and start shouting and swearing at you and find any excuse to attack you. I tried talking to them, I mean there was that girl who followed me home that time and punched me. I told her I'd never spoken to her before in my life and she reckoned I'd called her a slag which was really pathetic and she wouldn't leave me alone. She wouldn't leave it. Numerous people won't listen to you when you say 'What's your problem?' They just have a go at you even more. So you have to hurt them badly enough that they'll leave you alone, whether that's saying something nasty to them, hitting them or whatever.

So in what ways have you built your confidence up?

Living away from home, going to college and meeting people who didn't know anything about me, and just starting again. I just thought if people didn't like me 'So what, it's their loss!' I carried on being myself and had fun. You've got to help yourself, get out there and not rely on others to solve your problems for you. I suddenly had to solve all my problems without help from Mum and Dad and had to face them head on.

My friend Dan said to me that we humans are quite intellectual as individuals but thick in a group context. Do you think that's particularly true with bullies?

Definitely, they all follow the leader to be 'cool' and in with the gang.

Did being bullied give you any qualities as a person that help you now?

Yes, I won't take any abuse or let anyone boss me around. I'm a lot more confident and I like myself a lot more. I don't care what people think of me or whether they want to be friends with me or not because I know I can survive on my own.

Do you think that going through what you did was beneficial even though it was horrible at the time?

I guess so but I still can't see it that way. I still see it as an awful experience; it shouldn't have happened and shouldn't happen to anyone, but you need to put the past behind you.

Nigel White

Counsellor at Leeds Metropolitan University

What psychological impact does bullying have on a victim's life?

I think it has a big impact on their self-esteem. Somehow they have to come to terms with that picture of themselves as a victim. They also develop a tendency to bully themselves. They may have developed a stutter for example, and go to buy something, stutter and then beat themselves up for doing it. I think one of the worst effects of bullying is where the external event, e.g. the larger child knocking the small child out of the way on the playground, gets internalised and the victim sees themselves as less than worthy. That can last for years and years, long after the original external event itself.

Do you think that the solution then is to change the negative thoughts about yourself in your head to positive ones?

There are people who've successfully overcome incidents of bullying without going down that path of self-bullying. They're probably people who've got other resources at home. In an ideal situation the victim could go home and say such and such has happened to me today, and the parents will be supportive. These people have a really strong sense of themselves and will react to the incident and know that it's wrong, and will think about it in a way that's more helpful to themselves. A lot of people have great internal resources anyway, for example, if they've been shouldered out of the way, it doesn't seem to bother them. But how victims plan to help themselves out of that situation is a difficult question as is how society plans to help victims of bullying.

A lot of people hold this feeling of shame, e.g. 'I've been bullied, it's my fault.' When all this is bottled up it means that no one else can actually help you. No one knows what you're going through and the victims own external world will be very painful to them.

If you couldn't tell anyone or you told your mum and dad and they didn't help you, is it possible to solve the situation yourself?

I think given time that there are solutions. However, for a victim to find that person to find that solution can take an enormous amount of time. Especially if they're locked in a cycle of feeling ashamed. It's very difficult for them to access all the available resources if they're keeping everything so private. If the victim is prepared to open up and tell someone how bad they feel because they were bullied, then there's a possibility they may hear something supportive back.

A lot of bullied people will end up identifying with the bully, which is a horrendous situation to get into. As a way of resolving the conflict within themselves some victims see themselves as weak and have no sympathy for themselves. They see the person who was bullied as pathetic and weak and really want to be like the bullies, confident and strong. I think a lot of the macho element in our culture has a similar influence. We tend to look up to strong people.

Do you think bullies are strong people themselves?

Often not, they may have the physical strength to push someone over, but the motivation to do that could be fear or it could be the idea of a pecking order. The bully might think, 'I was bullied by the people older than me so now it's his turn. When I was at school, I couldn't see any reason why I was bullied except that maybe that's what happened to the people before me, so they in turn did it to me.'

Do you think fighting back physically should be a victim's last option?

You do hear stories of a child being bullied and they go home and are advised by their dad to hit back with the promise that it will end then. The child might go back and do this and sure enough people may change their attitude towards him or her because no one's going to pick on someone who can inflict some pain back. This approach is great as long as the kid can carry it off. If he goes back and tries to square up to the bully and makes a fool of himself then he's going to look even more vulnerable to the bullies. Your father, for example, can tell you to fight them but it's difficult because the victim himself is alone in the situation. To stand up to our fears is a very hard thing to do and maybe we spend our whole lives trying to do that.

Is the solution then to face your fears?

I don't think there's one solution to bullying. I think it's one solution that works sometimes. From a parent's point of view they should sit down and consider the kind of solution that would work for their child, because everyone is different. Some kids will respond better to understanding rather than the parents shouting, 'Stand up to them', because then you'll end up bullying your own child. It may be a case of doing enough to survive what is a difficult environment. Not every child is suited to the competitiveness of the school environment. They need to cope and get through it somehow with a sense of self worth. They may be better off keeping out of the bully's way and getting away to interests they enjoy more. I don't think encouraging every child to move up the pecking order is necessarily a brilliant idea. At many schools now, they have in place a peer-counselling scheme, which I think, is a good idea because it gets people thinking about things.

What do you think makes a victim?

I think it's situational; you could go to a school and predict which children are vulnerable to bullies. Certain situations are geared towards competitiveness. Schools encourage competitiveness; the whole culture we have is very encouraging of competitiveness. Bullying happens at the interaction between group processes and contextual events, a playground, for example, is a context. If you took away the context, bullying wouldn't happen. It has to be a playground, or a barracks, or a university or a bus queue. Bullying is the interaction between that context and the individual. I don't like the idea of blaming the victims; I think it puts too much emphasis on the individual. I think a lot of the responsibility for bullying rests upon our culture.

Dan Newbould

Assistant Boxing Coach

What do you think a victim lacks?

'It's just confidence and self-belief. I think you're vulnerable, especially as a teenager because you just want to be popular and you want everyone to like you. You take into account what people say too much and try and please everyone. But you learn in the end that it isn't worth it. As a teenager you speak to your parents and they say, 'Just be yourself and everyone will like you.' I remember thinking, 'I don't know who I am really, I'm growing up and changing all the time. I don't know what I want to be or how to act.' So you don't really know yourself well enough and you listen to other people far too much.

What a victim lacks is confidence and the self-belief that they're an all right person and that they're not what the bullies say they are. In my personal opinion, I think that everybody in the world can say they've been bullied at some stage in their life. It could be at school or a person could be bullied by their father. There is always a case where people have been bullied, whether it's mentally or physically.'

So you can distinguish between the two?

'Definitely. Physical bullying is preceded by mental bullying. Mental bullying is basically someone being abused vindictively by another person. But if you nip it in the bud straightaway and establish from the start that you won't be pushed around, then the bully will move on to another target. It comes down to self-belief and confidence. Do you actually believe what the bully is saying about you to be true? It's whether or not you have the strength to say 'No I'm not like that.'

Do you think physical and mental abuse always go together?

'I believe that if a person is getting physically abused, they're getting mentally abused as well. I believe you can have mental abuse without physical abuse, but not the other way around. Once you're being physically abused the bully has already got you and the solution to that is a very tricky question. I also think it's unlikely that the bullying will be done by just one person. Though it's something I never faced and I'm very glad about that.'

What do you think harms a person's self-esteem more: getting taunted or getting beaten up?

'You're led to believe that as a man you're supposed to be able to defend yourself. In all the films you have the hero, the guy that doesn't take any abuse off anyone. If you're getting beaten up, you already feel as though you're not a man. And this detracts from any confidence or self-belief that you have. Though I'd have to say that mental abuse is worse because a person can get stronger physically. But without the strength in your mind to not believe what the bullies are saying, you're in trouble.'

Do you think that a victim is on a downward spiral when they start listening to the bully's abusive comments?

'Yes, it is a downward spiral and the solution is to stop it the very first time it happens. If you let someone abuse you just one time then they're going to know that they can do it again. You've got to throw back any verbal abuse straight away or it's all over for you.'

How do you know then that very first time that people aren't joking and are in fact trying to bully you?

'You can tell from their posture; the way they speak to you will be more threatening. If they're not joking, they'll have a serious expression when they're taking the mickey out of you. If after say thirty seconds you stand up to them and they break out into a smile and say 'I'm only messing with you,' then you know it's just fun. But if it keeps going give them some abuse back. Don't give people the impression that you're just there to be shot at. In a group situation you should put the onus back on the loudmouth. If he's trying to show off to his mates and get everyone laughing at you, then say something back and put the pressure on him. Then it's up to him to react and you can read the situation from there.'

Do you think that a lot of bullying stems from the competition of the school environment?

'Yes, because everyone wants to be popular. Everyone wants to be heard and the quieter ones are normally the ones that get picked on. I was always quiet at school; the people I knew were all very loud. I remember being mentally bullied because I wasn't that loud. There's always one lad in every school who thinks he's a bit special and has a very quick mouth on him. You let them get away with it because it doesn't seem worth the hassle to deal with it.

When I was sixteen this one lad in my rugby team was always having a go at my girlfriend in class. But I didn't do anything about it and I can't to this day understand why, especially when a friend said 'Why didn't you wipe the floor with him?' My answer was that I thought I'd piss off all my friends in the team if I knocked out one of our best players. I learnt the lesson that it doesn't matter what anyone thinks, if someone's bullying you, you must not allow it. In that situation I should have dragged him out of the classroom and beaten the shit out of him. I think that would have worked quite well! If I could go back, that's what I would have done.'

Did you have the physical confidence to do it at that time?

'I played rugby and did a lot of weights. But I didn't really know how to handle myself in a fight. I'm a very easy-going character. I don't like fighting. I played rugby because everyone else did, it was the done thing and you got some recognition for doing it. But I didn't really enjoy the physical contact, so maybe I didn't have the confidence physically to do it. But with hindsight I could have done it, especially if I'd learned to box earlier, then I would have done it. To develop that confidence I'd advise people to learn to box. You need something simple and something that works. When you go to boxing three or four times a week you quickly learn how to throw punches. And you learn that getting hit doesn't actually hurt that much. It's a funny sensation getting hit; it's like a wake up call. Suddenly you're ten times more awake, your reactions are ten times quicker and everything switches on. I was terrified of getting hit but it's not as bad as you think it is. And then realizing this you're not as scared of getting into a confrontation like that.'

So really it's fear of a certain consequence that stops a victim fighting back?

'Yes, I was always very aware of this at school. I was worried about upsetting my parents and I was worried about the consequences of wiping the floor with the lad who kept picking on my girlfriend. He was our fly half and an important part of the team, so I was quite worried about knocking him out in case it upset the other lads on the team. You are always worried about consequences and I believe you should be because that's what keeps you civilized, knowing the difference between right and wrong. There is a consequence for every action you make in life.'

Do you not think then that it's wise for the victim to turn that fear of consequence around? They should be thinking 'If I confront the bully there will be a consequence. But if I don't confront the bully I'm going to continue leading an unhappy life?'

'You can turn it around, but I would have found that very hard to do on my own. Basically you just want it to go away. You think 'Maybe if I leave it he'll move on to someone else.' I don't believe that fear helps me to do anything, being angry does. If what someone does to you makes you angry it will make you do something about it. But it takes courage to do that because you basically want it to go away. So I say get angry and do something about it.'

But what if your self-esteem is so low you feel deserving of the bullying and can't get angry about it?

'If you have good parents then you can get guidance, but if they don't know what's going on then there's no guidance. And being on your own in that situation is very tough. If I hadn't had a friend who advised me afterwards I wouldn't have realized that I should have forgotten the possible consequences. The other lad started the situation by mouthing off at me, so I should have sorted him out. But I couldn't have realized this on my own, victims need guidance. If I'd read a book like this years ago it would have helped a lot. Bullying affects you more as a teenager because you've got more questions in your life that you're trying to answer. Your parents tell you it's the best time of your life, but they must have a really funny memory. They must only remember getting laid or drinking beer for the first time because there is so much shit that goes with being a teenager. You're growing up and thinking, 'Well how do I act now?' It's a big step from playing with Action Men to going through puberty. Suddenly every girl that walks past is attractive. Bullying is more detrimental at this stage because you're so unsure of yourself.'

Do you believe that a bully is selecting a victim to take part in a game for their own satisfaction?

'A bully is looking to feel a bit better about themselves. It's human nature that if you want to pick on someone you don't pick on the hard person, you pick an easy target. A bully feels better about themselves by making someone else suffer. Another big belief of mine I that as a race we are very advanced but when it comes down to it we have two urges: to fight and to procreate. If you walk down the street in any city, everyone seems to avoid eye contact, very few people will speak to someone they don't know and sat hello or whatever. People are scared of one another, scared of violence and of getting beaten up. If everyone could fight and defend himself or herself I think everyone would be much nicer to one another.'

So how useful do you think the physical training is?

'It's great because it gives you confidence and self-belief that you can look after yourself. It gives you an extra thick skin to anyone's comments because you know you could wipe the floor with them in a fight. I used to worry a lot about what other people thought of me: you try to laugh along with their jibes because you want them to like you. At school you can't get away from these people so you have to cope with it as best you can. Even the most popular people at school don't have an easy ride. Every situation is different though. I knew people who were very funny and that helped them avoid being bullied. You've got to find the key that works for you and physical training will help your confidence. If you're willing to stand up for yourself then the bully will not select you as a victim.'

If victims helped themselves and others gave encouragement to victims do you think bullying could be stamped out?

'In a perfect world, Rob, yes. There are cases of people standing up for victims for no reason other than out of the goodness of their own heart. But it could go one of two ways. You could either cause the bully to shrivel away or you could make an enemy that could lead to a physical confrontation. As a victim though you should always give the bully one warning and one warning only before you fight him. Repeated warnings only encourage the bully because you're not actually doing anything. But beating the bully is often an effective answer. It's a terrible thing to say because were supposed to be this advanced society who can do amazing stuff like walk on the moon and go into space. But in my personal opinion the best way to deal with a bully is to fight them and win.'

Tim Bartlett

School Headmaster

Are there many incidents of bullying at your school?

'It's a difficult question to answer in terms of actual offences. There are those that are reported and those that aren't. Bullying used to be entirely unreported or, if it was reported, ignored. There was a culture of teachers, I'm ashamed to say, who regarded bullying as part of growing up. They took the view that it didn't do them any harm and that it couldn't be stopped so the victims would just have to put up with it. That changed significantly fifteen years ago and the media had a large part to play. Organisations like Childline had a very high public profile.

Also in the early 1980s there was the abolition of corporal punishment in schools. Once it became impossible for teachers to hit children then the whole culture in schools started to shift. Teachers regained the moral high ground in terms of being aggressive because if teachers weren't physically aggressive then the students should not be either. That enabled us to deal more effectively with bullying. To draw an analogy, most schools are becoming non-smoking. And again it's about getting hold of the moral high ground because it's difficult to tell children over the age of sixteen not to smoke if the teachers do it. The bullying analogy goes back to the abolition of corporal punishment. Bullying in the workplace, amongst staff has also become an issue. So management styles which were macho, aggressive, uncaring and insensitive have become subject to debate. And of course it is now regarded as poor practice, there are actually harassment procedures in place for employees that almost exactly mirror bullying policy in schools.

Therefore both schools and workplaces are all pushing in the same direction. So what were saying is that this style of behaviour, mistreating people and misusing power to make somebody feel fear is unacceptable in society. In the family I don't doubt that severe physical chastisement by parents will be outlawed. I don't think it will be very long before the courts convict a parent of assault. Therefore it's a task for the schools that have rules that mirror the law to try and create a better, less violent society. Gandhi said that you have to be the change you want in the world. So if teachers want to stop bullying they first have to stop bullying the kids themselves. In terms of your question on how much bullying there is, I think there is too much in many schools. The only real target to aim for is zero.'

In what ways then can you deal with a bully?

'Well first of all I regularly put across to students that reporting incidences of bullying is a good thing to do and is protective of the school community. If we get a report of bullying there are several things we do. The victim needs reassuring firstly that it will stop, not immediately but it will stop now it's been reported. Secondly having asked a few sensible questions in 99.9% of cases the victim has done nothing wrong. And you need to keep reassuring them of that. They may have been in the wrong place at the wrong time, wearing the wrong t-shirt, glasses or the wrong designer label trainers. Anything can trigger it; it's not about moral fault it just happens.

With the bully it's a very similar process. We sit them

130

down, ask them what's been going on and tell them it's going to stop. It's simply a matter of asking whether they're going to stop now or if were going to have to keep working on them until it stops. You give them the same impression really, now that everybody knows about it it's going to stop. Victims are almost always in fear that reporting it will make matters worse. It doesn't matter how successful we are in stopping bullying the culture of fear simply remains. Even if we have a 100% record for stopping bullying, the very next student that reports it is still going to have that fear.

We always try to discover if the incident of bullying was seen by anyone else. We can give the impression then to the bully that a number of people have reported it. The bully gets the sense that other students are watching them. Or in other words the community is not on their side anymore.

I am very upfront in assemblies. I say things like 'We know that some people here are bullies don't we?' Most of the students sit absolutely still and won't even look up. It gives them the impression that everybody's watching the bullies. The true deterrent is making the bully realize that he or she can't get away with it.

What I hope is happening out there is that the one thing the students are certain of is that if they report bullying something happens, it is not ignored. People don't want bullies to be punished, in my experience: they simply want it to stop. We do have students who despite everybody's best efforts bully a succession of people. They're the people with the serious problems and its society that has the problem because these people may well become bullying partners in a marriage, bullies at work. However they are a very small minority, I could probably name those because their names keep coming up. The persistent appeal to their better judgement is what works with most. But placing the bullies in fear only validates their own strategy and behaviour.

These bullies need professional help that the school is unable to give. Their self-esteem is so low that it needs professional help beyond which a teacher can provide. They are a small minority and are what I would describe as 'personality bullies'.'

Does a victim's sense of shame also prevent many cases being reported?

'Yes, because despite what others say the victim often believes that it's their fault. There's a scene in the film 'Pretty Woman' that I like where the man tells the woman that she is very special and has special gifts. She replies that the bad stuff is easier to believe. It's true of most of us, we can be praised nine times and feel good about it. But if you're criticized once then it keeps you awake at night. Deep down in all of us is a guilt feeling that we are not worthy. Shame is a sense of humiliation that you've been made to fear.'

Would you say it was the victim's responsibility to solve it themselves?

'No, I think it's their responsibility to report it but that's their only responsibility. After that they need to get on with their lives whilst other people sort out what they've reported.'

How do you think a bully selects a victim?

'There are physical ways like a person wearing the wrong trainers, or being in the wrong place at the wrong time. It can be that the victim did something that 999 times out of a thousand has no consequences, e.g. taking someone's pencil without asking.'

What is your approach to a victim who retaliates physically to a bully?

'If the victim acts in complete self-defence when they're under threat then that's a complete defence of the victim. The sort of incidences were talking about are the times when someone retaliates and claims they were provoked. That doesn't relieve them from having done something wrong but what you do is temper the telling off with the circumstances. You'd tell them that violence is never right, that it doesn't solve anything. It hasn't made this situation better because now you've got into trouble with me. You tell the pupil that you understand why they did it but that it remains wrong. However there are grades of retaliation, a very serious assault does need punishing. If a bully pokes them and they turn round and lay them out cold they can't say 'Well he started it'. We can't condone violence because that would say 'It's all right as long as you've got enough power to overcome the person'. It is an acceptable answer if the victim acts in total self-defence; I've no problem at all with that.'

In what ways would suggest a victim could increase their confidence?

'Part of what schools do is raise people's self-esteem although some go beyond what we can offer. There are 'personality victims' as well as bullies. With pupils with low self-esteem we make sure they're achievements are praised and we temper any criticism. We encourage them to volunteer for something, or give them an award or commendation. We look for unobtrusive opportunities to help that person improve their self-worth. Many students who behave badly through bullying have low self esteem. They may be loud, difficult to deal with or 'in your face' and that's usually caused by low self-esteem.'

What advice would you give to parents whose child is being bullied?

'It's the most awful thing for a parent, the most terrible thing that can happen to a child in school. For a child to tell a parent they're being bullied and then to go to school with fear is a parent's worst nightmare. If the child discloses the problem to the parent that's good. Often parents feel guilty that they didn't know because kids are very good at hiding the fact they're unhappy. I'd advise parents to give their child opportunities to disclose, ask them how things are at school and if there is anything they should know. If the child discloses to the parent and they tell me then I can in all honesty tell the bully that I didn't find out through the victim. This helps protect the victim a bit and stops the bully going straight to them after seeing me.'

What psychological impact do you think bullying has on the victim?

'It's devastating. We mentioned physical bullying but I think the mental bullying is worse. Students are very knowledgeable about the normal give and take of school life. For example, the muttered insult under the breath or the shout down the corridor, finding someone's taken your pencil case again. They all know the hurly burly of school life and they all know where the boundaries interfere. Twenty years ago bullying was seen as the hurly burly of life.

The last thing I would like to say is that I don't think that court cases involving bullying are helpful to schools. But bullying does have a big impact on a person's life and they and their parents are seeking some form of compensation. The only body they can challenge is the school and whether it's been effective in preventing it. There are cases every year and there will be more, but that's not actually helping. I don't think schools needed reminding that the most important thing we do is to send students confidently out into the world. Schools are doing everything they can to combat bullying. If there is a case where a school is clearly negligent, where they have on anti-bullying policy and are still twenty years behind the times, then they should be in court. I wouldn't want my daughter to go to a school where they thought bullying was OK.

If schools become more cautious about the disclosures it may make bullying more difficult to detect. It may go back to only the students knowing about it. Schools may start to say they don't want to know about bullying if by knowing about it they are open to litigation. They might start saying 'Bullying is a matter for your parents' and wouldn't that be a disaster? What I hope is going to happen is that only the clearly negligent schools will be punished. For the rest of us who have children of our own and who are trying to create a generation of students who see bullying as out of date. In schools it should be taught that bullying is a facet of how school used to be. What I say to students is that when they're reading to their children in years to come and they come to the word 'bullying' they have to explain what it means because they would have no experience of it. I always say as well that bullying is something in their control. It's something young people do to other young people and is a problem we can do something about.'

Geoff Thompson

Author of
'Watch My Back – A Bouncer's Story'

What Are Your Thoughts on Bullies and Victims?

'Of course, like just about everyone else I dislike bullies and what they stand for. Although I do think there are different types of bully, some people are not even aware of the fact that they are bullies and would no doubt deny emphatically that they are. One of my early bullies, on reading about himself in my book 'Watch My Back', actually rang me up distraught because I had named him as my bully. He said that he could remember nothing at all about bullying others. In fact his one dominant memory from his school days was that he was bullied himself.

So it is very easy to generalize and say how bad and malicious these people are and it is very easy to de-humanise them. But, as I said, as much as we may dislike them, they are still human and often their bullying is, whilst hurtful, often inadvertent. Often it is an act of displacement because they themselves are being bullied. This doesn't make it right but it goes some way to understanding the mechanics of it all.

As for the victims, I was one. I think that people only treat us how we allow them to treat us. Whilst it is often frightening to confront a bully at school, in the home or the workplace, it is something we need to do if we ever want to stop the abuse. When I say 'stop the bully' I don't necessarily mean beat him up or violently attack him or her. What I mean is we need to stand our ground, even if it is only to say 'Do you realize that you are bullying me and that it is making me extremely unhappy?' This one statement can go a long way to solving your problems because I believe that until these people are told that what they are doing is actually abuse they may not, on a conscious level know it. So if we don't like the bullies, if we don't like the abuse, then we have to dig deep and do something about it or it will follow us from place to place.'

What do you think is a victim's answer to bullying?

'A victim's answer to bullying is whatever he wants it to be. It is a very subjective matter. What I find an entirely reasonable answer may well be completely unacceptable to someone else. As individuals we must seek an individual answer that suits us as people. What I would say is that we must stand up to bullies verbally or through an official channel (if the bullying is in the workplace.) If we do nothing to solve our problems then our problems are unlikely to change. I understand why people do not stand up to their problems. I know that they are scared, but there is help out there for those that ask.'

What stops a victim from fighting back?

'Fear. People are frightened that if they fight back their problems will increase. What people often don't realize is that if they don't stand up to their abusers their problems will increase anyway. If they do stand up for themselves there is a very healthy chance that their problems will dissipate. As I said it is very sobering to be told that you are a bully and that you are abusing others, because no one wants to see themselves as abusive. So until someone tells them they will probably not recognize it on a conscious level. I worked on a course with about twenty other trainees. The manager of the course was a bully, even though he never acknowledged it.

I made it my duty to stand up to this man, as did all the other trainees bar one. We all signed a petition and handed it to the top man at the centre and said that we were no longer going to put up with the abuse. We all risked our jobs in doing so, but who wants a job where the boss is an abusive bully anyway. As it turned out the petition did the job, he quietened down and left us alone. I mean when nineteen people sign a petition saying they are unhappy with your attitude you have to start asking yourself questions. We probably did him a favour, made him look a little closer at himself. I hope we changed him for the better. At the very least we changed his attitude towards us.'

What do you think makes a victim stand out to a bully?

'Normally a bully will escalate his abuse. He will try getting away with a little abuse and if you let him, that abuse will escalate until you become a slave to his abuse. As I said, sometimes that escalation is so subtle that even the bully doesn't realize the full extent of his abuse. I have seen it with friends who talk to their partners like they are rubbish. I said to one of my friends 'I can't believe you talk to your wife like that, it's terrible.' He said 'What?' He had become so used to his ways that he didn't even know what he was doing.

Another friend told his wife that he was tired of her attitude to him, but she flatly denied that she had even raised her voice. He made a recording of her one day, without her knowing and played it back to her, she was devastated. What she heard on the tape, the tone as much as the words, devastated her because she never really saw herself in that way. Bullying can be very subtle, often inadvertent but always hurtful, often fatal. People need to be told when they abuse, whether it is on the school playground, on the shop floor or in the workplace. If we do not stand up to them then we have no right complaining about them. Sitting with your mates talking about the cruelty of your boss just does not cut the mustard. These people need confronting and telling in no uncertain terms that what they do is abuse and not acceptable.'

Is it the victim's responsibility to sort the problem out themselves?

'Yes. If they don't who will? Who can? People may offer advice, they may point the way, but no one can do it for you. The problem with bullying is that if you don't put a stop to it yourself at some point it is always going to follow you.'

Can a victim overcome bullying without fighting back physically?

'As far as I'm concerned fighting back physically is not the answer except in such circumstances that you have no other option. Even then it is an individual choice. Not everyone can get their head around physical violence. Most people, from my experience, couldn't fight back even if they wanted to; they simply haven't developed the skill. So for me communication is the key, talking situations out or down, getting around the negotiation table. Physical violence is lower echelon communication. We should only go there if there is absolutely no other choice and even then we must expect a karmic unfolding.

There are consequences: police involvement, comebacks, etc, that accompany violence that are often more unpleasant than the bullies we have attacked. We should face our abusers and use verbal communication to problem solve.'

If you could teach one physical technique to a victim what would it be?

'Firstly I always teach people to avoid, escape, use verbal dissuasion, loophole, and posture, run away if you can. If all this fails and you have no other option but a physical response and you choose that option – hit hard with a punch and hit first. The pre-emptive attack is the only thing I find works consistently. So in one line 'learn to hit f***ing hard'. If you do use a physical response make sure you are aware of the law. You may have to defend your right to self-defence in the courts.'

Reuben Cole

Residential Social Worker

As a social worker do you see many incidences of bullying?

'The people involved where I work do have considerable difficulties integrating with others in society. The kids I supervise all want to achieve a certain level in the hierarchy: they want to be the joker or they want to be the hard man.

They want to act a certain part and all the bullying I've seen has occurred when a third party has become involved. The third child might be higher in the hierarchy and one might want to be closer to him. So suddenly, without provocation this kid will start. Bullying can happen in the playground, the pub or in this case with these kids who are all thrown into the stewpot together.

They're all trying to be part of the hierarchy. Nobody wants to be at the bottom and everybody wants to be at the top. There will always be one kid who is top dog and one who is at the bottom.'

Do you try then to re-educate the bully about their behaviour? Or are you more interested in helping the victim acquire confidence?

'It's a case of trying to do both really. The way society is set up it seems that the weaker will always get trampled on. We try to teach the victims to learn to speak out and alert the teacher in the classroom, the social worker on call, or their parents. Anyone really who won't say 'I'm going to hit you, I'm going to put you past the level that you're making me feel'.

I think it's important that parents take their kids aside and actually tell their kids what bullies are. They are people who are uncertain about themselves and to cover up for that they'll be violent, for example. That's their substitute for a lack of confidence in themselves. The only way they can feel together with themselves is by putting other people down. But all the children have down days, where they'll feel like a victim in some way. A bully will make up for this feeling by proving that they're wittier than someone else or stronger or that they can drink more beer or whatever.

From my perspective the bottom line is that both bullies and victims need adjusting. In terms of transforming a victim I don't think I've seen anyone go from being a victim to someone not afraid of bullies, without becoming a bully themselves. With the bully it's a case of teaching them new values.'

Who do you see as the bigger problem, the bully or the victim?

'That's a hard question to answer because although the bully is the one causing all the pain. The victim tends to become so trampled upon that they almost let it happen. The problem is that if the victim goes to the authorities they may get bullied even more because the bully found out that they told.

The only way I can see bullying being stopped at school or in a residential setting is by proper supervision of the bullies. It's important also to get home to the victim

142

the message that they're not weak or weird. It is the bully who has the problem.'

How does a bully select a victim?

'First of all the bully will seek out someone he sees as inferior. Just as a paedophile looks for a child he'll look for someone who hasn't got the power to fight back. Secondly he'll look for someone who isn't going to be rallied around. If he tries to bully someone by calling them a name and all the 'victim's' mates rally round him then there will be a dissolution of the bullying. A bully stalks his or her victim and once they've been targeted the bully will come back again and again. Usually in the first instance a bully will be with friends or some cushion so they won't have to fight if the first approach goes wrong. After the first couple of incidents the victim's morale starts to dissolve and you get children who won't go to school. I've had kids attack me and it's not down to them being upset at me, it's because they're scared to go to school. A bully is nothing more than a makeshift predator. If he's regulated by his friends, school or family then the chances are he or she will stop.'

Is it the victim's responsibility to sort it out themselves?

'Really I think this idea reflects upon the male psyche. From the media and other sources males feel that they have to deal with it themselves. And they often expect to deal with it physically. People say that bullies are cowards. Yes they are cowards but a group of five or six cowards is a lot for a victim to handle. An incidence of bullying should be dealt with by the regulation forces before it develops any further. The victim should alert the authorities but also let the bully know, ideally by non-violent means that they are not going to be pushed around. I have seen victims stand firm and say something witty back to get the bully's mates laughing at the bully.

A bully is like a professional thief. He or she is not going to try to mug a large, confident looking person because it makes for a lot of work. A bully doesn't want to work for his victims, he wants it to be easy. The solution for the victim is to make the bully's work difficult for him. At work I've witnessed child A attack child B. Child B (the victim) kicked back at child A and I saw fear in child A's eyes. I could see him thinking 'Oh God, I've got a fight on my hands now. I thought I could get away with it.' He looked scared and that's the way bullies are. They might try again a couple more times to make sure the victim's reaction wasn't a failure, but sooner or later they'll back off.'

Is there a point where even the scared victim will fight back?

'Yes, in my experience a child has three levels to deal with bullies. The first level involves talking back. The second level they get more aggressive and at the third level they kick off. I've seen cornered children snap and go straight to level three and fight. However I believe that a victim needs to deal with it rationally and think of ways to solve it first without fighting.'

How do you help kids who are so held back by fear and shame that they feel unable to fight back?

'With kids who've experienced a lot of bullying you can see the absolute fear in their eyes. When the bully walks in the room and sees that fear he or she acknowledges that as respect. Therefore the bully will continue with their behaviour. However if an adult or another authority intervenes and gives the victim a breathing space then with time and a lot of talking you can help. You can reassure them of all the things they've suspected to be true but haven't believed. Namely that the bully is a coward and is the one with the true problem.'

In your job do you try to get across the message that life is too short to be unhappy?

'I work with children in care and they have a lot of other problems anyway. But with bullying the best way is to try to talk to people you have a grievance with. Talk to them, ask them if they wouldn't mind doing something about it. Life is too short to try and prove to someone that you're more dominant than them. I'd rather prove to somebody that I was fun to be with than prove I was 'great' because I made another person feel small. I'd rather crack a few gags about drinking four pints and not being able to take it any more than trying to make out I'm hard because I can drink fourteen.

Passivity is a great way to be. If you don't like somebody that's fair enough but don't try to use it as tool to gain false friends in the way bullies do.'

Why do you think bullies have false friends or hangers-on?

'Basically because they're looking for someone to aspire to be. The social construction of the bully begins as a child. A child wants a social model. An identity. On their first day at school they meet lots of kids they don't know. They want these kids to like them so they find themselves a role in the peer group. Some kids will be funny or stylish or whatever. But one kid will be the 'hard' one and he'll have people following him who also aspire to that 'hard' identity.'

Is bullying then down to insecurity and people seeking identity?

'Absolutely. Some people might not know any other way. Their Dad might be violent towards their mother and they see it as a way of life. They see it as a way of conveying affection and see it as acceptable.'

As a social worker do you feel any responsibility towards doing something about bullying?

'Yes I feel a great obligation to contribute. I put up a common sense barrier with the kids. If one of them is a bully I'll tell them so. When the bully does not gain the acceptance of someone who's approval they want they tend to change their ways. Like a girl who goes out with a lad who hits her and she stays with them. It's the worst thing she can do. She's sending a message to the lad that his behaviour is acceptable. The best thing for people to do if they know a bully is to ditch them. Then they won't have friends in the peer group and will have to re-think their identity.'

What do you think of the theory that bullying is a form of secret society? Is the answer to get the problem out in the open?

'Bullies have an almost colonial attitude. They say to the victim 'I'll take what I want and you'll be thankful for it.' The victim is the bully's food. Without a victim a bully can't function, however they will retain that certain mentality. It is a very secret society. If it became open at one or both ends then it would cease to be. If the secret society is not maintained because the victim tells someone who can help then the bullying will not continue.'

Is a bully's success often because they strike a raw nerve with the victim?

'I don't think a bully succeeds so much because of that, because in my view a victim is very likely to fight back if the bully strikes a raw nerve. I think it's more a case of the victim denying that they're being bullied. After a victim is insulted in the same way two to three times a day they might start to believe it to be true. Once it begins to affect the victim's self-esteem the bully has them and the bullying takes less work. I believe that the bully relies upon the victim more than vice versa. The victim is the bully's conversation, his joke, his punchbag. If the victim has a day off school what's the bully going to do? They can't form another relationship straight away because of the risk involved. To conclude I think there are only two ways to stop bullying. Firstly if the bully stops or secondly if the victim gains confidence in themselves.'

Gavin Jasper

Ex-amateur Boxer

Why did you define yourself as a bully? In what ways did you used to bully people?

As part of a group we would victimise people we saw as 'sad'. This would not usually include physically beating people up, but would be more verbal abuse and throwing people in showers, running away from them if they were out with us, etc, leaving them alone in town and hiding from them.

Were you aware that you were bullying people at the time?

Probably yes, but I thought that by being OK to people later in the day, then it would be alright.

Did you see bullying as a way to make yourself more popular or confident?

I was mainly part of a group, so I guess it was to make the other lads laugh and feel part of the group.

Was there ever a time when someone you were bullying stood up to you?

Yes, but that's when it would turn physical and people

generally backed down before a fight started, but there were always exceptions.

What did you think about the people you bullied?

Nothing really.

Were you ever bullied yourself? And did this lead you to bully?

I was bullied in my junior school by a lad I eventually became friends with (but only after a couple of scraps). That's the reason I never really took it too far.

Why did you stop bullying?

Just grew out of it. The whole group grew up and realised that it was a part of life we had to leave behind, but there are other books to be written about that! In Sixth form with another lad, we used to get kids who were being, or thought they were being bullied come to us and we would 'deal' with the bully – it usually worked.

Do you have a message to pass on to bullies and victims?

Bullies – have a look at yourself. You are probably weak alone and need to recognise this. The worst people in bullying are the people who are impressed by it. Without these people it would never go on.

Victims – always just walk away. Always tell someone and make a note of everything. Bullies will always be embarrassed when confronted by what they have done and when asked to explain it.

Ex-Bully (Name with held)

Why did you define yourself as a bully? In what ways did you used to bully people?

I never used to take money or anything like that, just used to take the piss out of the same people in particular lessons. I was not a physical bully in the sense that I used to hit people. It was more a case of putting people down a lot.

Were you aware that you were bullying people at the time?

I never really thought of myself as a bully as there were usually 2-3 people that would be involved in the bullying, and so we just thought it was a bit of a laugh. Plus, as I mentioned, I was never one to actually hit people or anything like that. And I suppose at the time my definition of a bully was someone who would beat other kids up for their dinner money etc.

Did you use bullying as a way to make yourself more popular or confident?

I suppose so, yes. At the time it was easy to make people laugh by putting other people down, especially the ones that didn't say anything back.

Was there ever a time when someone you were bullying stood up to you? If not, what would have been your reaction if anyone had?

There were quite a few times that people would talk back and try to get involved in a battle of words, if you like. But as there were always 2-3 of us, they would usually just go quiet, I assume in the hope that we'd grow bored of them and leave them alone.

What did you think about the people you bullied?

I never really thought much about it. I just thought it was a laugh. I never really thought about how those people probably dreaded seeing me in a lesson or a school corridor.

Were you ever bullied yourself? And did this lead you to bully?

I was never bullied. I was lucky enough to have an older brother and his friends who were always a few years above me at school. Plus, I was in a large cliquey crowd of what you might call the 'in crowd' at school, so I can honestly say I was never bullied, although I received a few slaps in my time!

Why did you stop bullying?

I think I just grew up. I started concentrating more in lessons rather than messing around, and also actually go to know the people I used to pick on, one of whom I regularly go out with at weekends with the same group of friends who used to join me in picking on him. We kind of laugh about it now, although at times you can see the embarrassment in both me and my friends when some of the stories are re-told.

Do you have a message to pass on to bullies and victims?

I can't really think of one to be honest. Needless to say, that the main reason I did it was to show off in front of friends. A lot of the time, I just didn't think for a minute that it was really having an effect. To those people that bully, but perhaps don't think they do, I would say that they should have a thought for how those being bullied feel every single time they see you. I'd also say that as people grow up, the tables could turn. Payback's a bitch!!

Chapter 12

Interview Conclusions

Having interviewed a wide cross-section of people I think it would be helpful to draw some general conclusions.

Everyone interviewed agrees that victims lack confidence and self-belief in themselves. However Dave Turton made the interesting point that bullies also lack confidence and are in fact 'victims of themselves.' Reuben made the point that at school all kids are seeking an identity. Many of them are insecure and this can lead them to bully, or at least follow the leader of a gang who is a bully.

Nigel commented that often bullies are taking their place in a 'pecking order'. This means that they were bullied by those older than them and are merely continuing the cycle by bullying those younger.

One of the main conclusions was that it is the bully who is the problem. They have the low self-esteem that leads them to make others suffer. Geoff Thompson made the point that often bullying is an 'act of displacement' by the bully because they are being bullied themselves. Everyone seems agreed upon the bully's ability to select the weakest, least confident member of a group for a victim.

Everyone agreed that a victim lacks self-confidence and self-belief. In Dan's opinion victims give other people's opinions too much power and are often hurt by them. Emma mentioned that a big factor in leaving the 'victim state' for her, was learning to like herself again after being bullied. Nigel added that a victim sabotages their own self-esteem because they beat themselves up over their weaknesses.

Dave made the point that victims often lack confidence when it comes to social interaction with others. As a result they stand out in a group situation because they are quiet. Dan said that he was quiet at school and that it made him a target for one particular lad. I would agree because I was quiet in group situations at school and was marked out as a victim.

In terms of responsibility for stopping the bullying, both Dave and Dan agreed that bullying needs stopping by the victim right from the very first incident. Leaving it any longer only makes it worse for the victim. Dan made the important distinction that bullying occurs when there's a joke or a comment made to someone and only one side is laughing. If both people enjoy the joke then that's fine.

Tim disagreed and said that it is not the victim's responsibility to solve the problem. He stated that it is the victim's responsibility to 'report' the bullying. By doing this the bully can be dealt with by the proper authorities. Reuben made a similar point when he said 'A bully is nothing more than a makeshift predator. If he's regulated by his friends, school or family then the chances are he'll stop.'

Geoff said that the victim has the responsibility to sort out the problem because nobody else can be relied upon to do it for them. Dave compared the bully to a snarling dog. If the victim faces getting bitten by the dog then it is the victim's responsibility to sort it out. However Dan made the point that guidance and encouragement is necessary as it is a very hard problem to solve alone.

On the question of responding to bullying by fighting the bully, there were differing opinions. Geoff said that a victim should do everything possible to solve the situation without fighting. Reuben agreed that a non-violent solution is best and Tim said that violence is never right. Nigel made the point that a physical response may well stop the bullying, but the victim has to be proficient enough to do it. Geoff added that fighting back would not be the answer for everyone. This approach did work for Emma, so you can see that whatever solution you choose will have to be right for the individual.

Everyone agreed that it is fear that stops a victim fighting back, though Nigel made the great point that standing up to our fears is a hard thing to do. Everyone agreed that the fear the victim has is a fear of a certain consequence. Both Dan and Emma reported being afraid of getting into trouble for fighting and in Emma's case she was at first afraid of getting hurt. I think this is where physical training is so important. As Dave said in his interview placing the victim under physical and emotional stress in training can help them overcome their fears and turn the situation around. Dan also made the great point that when you get angry at a bully you forget totally about your fear. The correct physical training will definitely teach you to develop that aggression. Nigel said that an ability to inflict pain on a bully would stop his behaviour. The experiences Emma recounts in her interview back this up.

Nigel concluded that there is no one solution to bullying that is set in stone. It is a case of a victim needing to find a solution that works for them. This opinion is backed up by Geoff, who said that a victim's answer to bullying is whatever he or she wants it to be. Dave noted that the best solution is to stop the bully in their tracks from the start with non-aggressive, non-compliance to any commands. If the bully tells you to fetch them something and you tell them to do it himself or herself, the bully may well move on. Reuben also said that a victim should seek 'non-violent' means of communicating to the bully that they won't be pushed around. Dave advised trying to make friends with the bully or at least find out why they're doing it. Emma tried this approach and it didn't work for her, but it may do for you. It is clear that each individual case is different.

Dave advised that it is better to avoid expecting the teachers or whoever to stop the bully. Besides the victim will gain confidence from sorting it out themselves. And as you can see from Emma's interview, you can't always rely upon teachers to believe you, never mind help you. So to sum up the victim should not, as Nigel said, bottle up their emotions. They should seek a solution immediately.

The main things to do are, as Emma and Dan said, try to let go of the need for people's approval and learn to like yourself. Train yourself physically to beat the bullies. As Emma found out and Dave advised, it's worth a telling-off at school if all other solutions fail and you have to beat the bully in a fight.

Each interview was great and very insightful. But I think the overriding opinion that came across is that a victim must find their individual solution. Bullying does destroy people's lives, therefore the victim should try the suggested solutions and keep trying until one of them works, whatever the consequences.

Chapter 13

Review Of Possible Solutions

Each bully and each situation is individual and will require an individual answer. In my experience I was victimized mainly by 'career bullies'. However there were some one-off incidents. I remember sitting in the canteen at school with my mates. This lad came over and sat down with us. He noticed that the door was open and said to me aggressively 'Shut door for me'. I said 'No. Do it yourself.' He didn't say or do anything else because he had tested the water and found it not to his liking. Most of the bullying I experienced and personally witnessed was mental in origin. I experienced very, very little physical bullying; it was mainly threats and verbal abuse.

This requires a different solution because although it is an attack on your person, it is not violent and does not require you to be fighting anyone. I think the best solution is to sigh, talk to the bully and tell them how weak they are, or to involve a third party such as a teacher.

Physical bullying requires a different answer, though. Again you should alert the school authorities so they can discipline the bullies. Then you can train your self-defence skills so you cannot be physically bullied again. Remember that if you attacked physically by a bully or if the bully has a history of violence and you feel under threat of attack, you have the right to self-defence.

I have read a great deal on the subject of violence and fighting back against bullies. And there seems to be a great deal of contention over whether a victim hitting a bully is right. Does it serve only to validate the bully's aggression? Does it only increase the amount of violence in the world?

In my opinion, yes it does increase the amount of violence and I guess it does validate the bully's aggression. But in many cases hitting a bully will stop their behaviour. It is an answer, perhaps not the most desirable one, but it is an answer. And when you're being bullied and at your wits' end nobody is justified in blaming the victim.

When I talk about fighting I'm not talking about someone in a pub fighting because someone spilt their drink. What I'm talking about is a person, whose life is being made a misery, trying to solve the problem in any way they can. I definitely advise trying to solve the problem by non-violent means, by being assertive and by telling the bully their behaviour is upsetting you.

Stopping the bullying this way is highly desirable. But I'd like to ask you a question. How can you appeal to a bully's good-natured side if they don't have one? You might for example, say to a bully *'Leave me alone, you're upsetting me'* and they might smirkingly reply, *'I know, I like it'*. So what do you do if you report the bullies and the teachers accuse you of causing the problems, as happened to my sister? What do you do if you're cornered by a gang of bullies and you can't get away?

Bullying is something you as a victim have to find an answer for and if in the situations above, that answer is hitting the bully then so be it. In the majority of situations we are talking about a frightened victim who just wants the bully to stop. I was once being harassed by a bully while a teacher stood by and watched. I kept telling him 'Leave me alone' and walking away, but he kept following me. A gang of bullies surrounded my sister, she couldn't get away and because she didn't hit the girl who was picking on her, she got hurt. Read the work of people like Geoff Thompson, Jamie O'Keefe and Dave Turton. When it comes to self-defence their experiences are proof that when cornered attacking first is the only thing that works.

Hitting a bully should be a last resort. If you've told them to leave you alone, you've reported them to the teachers and the bullying has continued. If you've tried to walk away but they've followed you then I see nothing wrong in hitting them. If someone is so intent on bullying you that hitting them is the only way to get them to stop I don't believe a victim should be seen as a wrongdoer.

This approach was a solution for me once on a bus after a school football match. The lad behind me kept punching the headrest of my chair and slapping the back of my head. I turned round and told him to stop it but he continued. Again I told him to leave me alone, he stopped but then did it again. So I turned round and punched him. That stopped him and he had nothing to say except 'You've made my nose bleed now.' He never bothered me again and in this instance a 'physical response' worked for me.

I personally disagree with the idea that a victim hitting a bully will make them as bad as the bully, or will make them a bully themselves. In a minority of cases it may do, but I believe in the majority of cases a victim just wants the bully to leave them alone. They have no desire to fight or make hitting people a regular past time. They may just do it out of desperation and once the bully has been stopped they are happy. In the situation I described above, I had no desire to fight my schoolmate. I just wanted him to leave me alone to enjoy the bus ride home. If a bully makes a victim so upset and distressed that they hit out, then in my opinion the bully deserves it.

To sum up here are the main solutions and points to remember about bullying:

1. Remember that you are not at fault for being bullied. Accept no blame and do not in anyway beat yourself up mentally for what happened. The bully is to blame, not you.
2. Remember that you have a choice about bullying. There are answers available and they will work if, as for an exam question, you prepare for the next attack.
3. Tell someone you trust about your predicament. Don't bottle up any anger or misery you feel at your treatment.
4. Learn to like yourself and let go of the need for the approval of other people.
5. Train the thoughts that enter your head. Don't allow your mind to dwell on anything negative or upsetting.
6. Try to solve the problem yourself first. Exhaust all your other options. If you're still being bullied, particularly if it's by a group of people, tell a trusted teacher at school and make them take the problem seriously.
7. Be aware of the competitive nature of your environment. Whether it's a classroom, office or sports club, be aware that in any group there will be bullies. Be prepared to repel the very first attack by anyone that feels like bullying. By being confident the very first time a bully tests the waters you may in fact put off many other attempts and save yourself a lot of trouble.
8. Do one small task every day that challenges you in order to build your self-esteem.
9. Train your physical skills until you are able to defend yourself automatically, without thinking about it.
10. As a last resort, dealing out physical pain to the bully should work. Remember the worst consequence that could occur with bullying is not you getting hurt or

getting into trouble. The worst possible consequence is for you to lose your self-esteem and have your life destroyed.

11. Remember the statistics at the beginning. You are not alone in being bullied; thousands of others also undergo the same treatment in schools all over Britain.

12. People do unfortunately commit suicide because of bullying. Don't allow things to get you to that stage. Be proactive. Take some form of action and responsibility for solving the problem. Do whatever it takes to sort it out.

Chapter 14

Committing To Change

To cement your commitment to a better life you could write down your plan. Here is an idea for a contract you can fill in, sign and date and start taking action now in phasing out the bullies in your life. Having a written record will make you more likely to succeed.

I *name* am committing myself, on the *date* to a happier life free from bullying.

I am no longer prepared to tolerate the misery and unhappiness bullies bring to my life. There is something wrong with them, not me. They are the ones with the problem and I no longer want them in my life.

These are the skills and techniques I'm going to learn in order to become a stronger person. *Write a description of exactly how you will do this and how often you will work at it.*

I realise that transforming my life in this way will be hard work. It may be especially difficult to start with but I know that every time I do not allow myself to be bullied I will get stronger and happier.

These changes will push me emotionally and there will be times when I am scared and want to just give up and stay a victim. But I will not ever give up. These changes are vital to me enjoying my life to the full.

In kicking bullying out of my life I am in fact saving my life because otherwise I will continue to live in misery.

I can and will lose the influence of bullies from my life.

Signed *Your signature*

Making this agreement with yourself should prove invaluable when you are scared and feel like giving up. Having made the commitment to yourself should inspire you to not give up whatever happens.

Chapter 15

How To Make Your Anger Work For You

Historian Francis Fukuyama in his book 'The End of History and the Last Man' described self-esteem as 'An innate human sense of justice.' He added that 'People believe they have a certain worth and when people treat them as though they are worthless, they experience the emotion of anger.' Fukuyama also said that when people allow their self worth to be undervalued they experience shame. It's very important that you don't allow yourself to feel ashamed at being bullied. Don't treat any feelings of shame as a negative thing; instead accept the message that the feeling is trying to give you. It's trying to make you realize that you are worthy of a better life than you currently have. You feel ashamed because you know that what people are doing to you is wrong. So use the energy from that feeling and take action to stop the bullying.

I feel it's a safe bet that along with the shame you also feel anger at your situation. So you're angry? Good. That means you're unhappy at being bullied and you're halfway to a sharp u-turn in life towards happiness. In his interview later in the book, Dan mentioned that anger is perhaps an even more powerful motivator than fear. This is especially true when it comes to resolving your problems with a bully. By letting go of the misconception that being bullied is your fault, you can learn to express your anger at the bully's behaviour. The step between wanting to change and actually changing is probably represented as a huge step by your mind. However the only thing stopping you now is the tissue paper thin, wall of fear.

To break through this wall you need to use the emotions that being bullied has given you. Use your anger at the situation to inform a trusted schoolteacher or use your anger to answer the bully back. Next time you're picked on don't hold your anger inside and feel sad, let it all out and do something to stop the bullying. Let the bullies know you're not happy with them. If the bully is aggressive towards you, making you scared, get angry with them for making you feel scared and defend yourself. The ability to get yourself into a state of aggression when facing a possible attack from a bully will be invaluable to you because you will not be stopped from defending yourself by fear. In fact if you are so annoyed at someone's behaviour towards you and you see the red mist, its unlikely you'll stop to think about being scared.

One of the few times I saw red and forgot about my fear illustrates this point well. One day after a football game this lad from school rode past me missiling spit in my direction as he went. Normally when this sort of thing occurred I would carry on as if nothing had happened. I would freeze with fear and this would prevent any anger or positive action from surfacing. If he'd just insulted me I might not have got angry but being spat at was too much, on this occasion I forgot all about my fear.

Before my best mate knew what was happening I was off down the road and had caught up with this lad. I remember spitting at him and landing a weak jab in his eye. He asked the usual question, (familiar to all in these parts) '*are you starting?*' (Obviously being punched in the face was not confirmation enough!) We both got off our bikes and I remember for a second thinking 'F**k he's big', so I hit him again. To my amazement, he ran down the driveway of this house. So I followed him, temper totally out of control and kept hitting him until to my surprise he began cowering and shouting for his mates. I was as happy as a man can be while still keeping his trousers on. This time the bully didn't get away with his behaviour because I used my anger and was not stopped by my very real fear of being unable to defend myself and of getting beaten up.

Anger is a very powerful motivator and if you use it properly you can achieve great things. However if you use your anger in the wrong way however it will only hold you back in life. Holding your anger in makes you ill inside, especially if you do this twenty-four seven as I once did. I felt anger at the bullies and even more anger at myself for allowing it to happen and for being so quiet and shy and not standing up to people.

What worked for me was to use my anger to help myself; the time of my GCSE exams is a great example. I was suffering the worst of the bullying at this time and as my way of showing everyone that I wasn't worthless I set about my revision program. At school I loved PE and history but that was about it, in spite of this I started to revise for two hours a night. I kept this up every school night and every weekend for four months. This was totally unheard of for me but I was so angry and determined to do well that I persevered. I also had to contend with my otherwise well meaning Dad, who would burst into my room most nights and shout and scream at me claiming I wasn't working hard enough and would 'End up stacking shelves in Asda.' Enduring this only made me more determined because now I wanted to show him how good I was too. When results day came around I surprised everyone, not least myself with great results in all of my eight subjects.

My anger also came in handy when I wanted to build

up my body because at age fifteen to sixteen I kept growing in height whilst staying clothes line thin. One of my main bullies commented on this in PE one day. He was a lot bigger than I was but unfortunately for him, had only a peanut for a brain. He looked at me and said sarcastically 'You're muscley aren't ya? ha ha'. After this I started weight training determined to build myself up. Every time I picked up a barbell or dumbbell and thought 'I can't lift this' I would see him in my mind and hear him laughing at me and suddenly the weight was easy to lift. That one comment that aimed to hurt me actually gave me three years of progress in my training and by the age of eighteen I had built myself up to the point that I was extremely happy with my body.

Using my anger positively has brought me a great deal of success, but if I had used my anger improperly I could have gone down the wrong road in life. In everyday life I see a lot of examples of angry people using their anger to hurt, rather than improve their lives. I see gangs of kids walking about fixing people with angry stares, shouting abuse, challenging people they've never met with the classic 'What's your f**king problem?' I see smashed up phone boxes, cars, property and I know that anger is the likely cause. I sigh every time I see this because the person who's done it has not used their anger to help themselves. They've used it in a way that won't do anything to improve their situation.

Sometimes I think people treat others badly because they were treated badly themselves. Perhaps unconsciously they want to make another person understand their situation and the pain they felt. It's as if they are hurting people and saying, 'Now do you see how it feels? It's not nice is it? Do you understand what I went through?' What this is really about for me is people being irresponsible with their anger by taking it out on others. Happiness is all about effective communication… communicating well with others and just as importantly… with yourself. It's about stripping down your emotions and being honest with yourself about how you really feel. When you break things down like this you almost sigh with relief because you're not hiding your real feelings. You're not hiding behind depression where you try not to feel anything at all, or anger where you get aggressive to hide your hurt. How many times have you seen a girl out with a new boyfriend and seen her ex-boyfriend lose his temper and get violent because he's hiding from the hurt he feels at seeing her with someone other than him?

I know all about anger, I lived in a cocoon of it for a few years, now I'm happier because I'm responsible with it, I'm honest with myself. I don't hide behind my anger, go out and get pissed on 8 pints of lager and smash up a car or a phone box or even, another person. That doesn't mean that I don't feel anger… we all do. What I have always done is use my anger to help myself, I get really determined and direct my anger into working towards whatever it is I want in my life.

If you feel full of anger and are hiding behind aggression and violence because you aren't living the life you want to there is a better way. Be honest with yourself and use all that angry energy, put it to use in the direction of whatever it is you think will improve your life. If you despise your job and you often give up with trying to get another then use your anger. Get determined and go out and achieve what you want too. Anger is just energy, you can use it wrongly to destroy things or use it in the best possible way which is to build things… build the life you want for yourself.

Anger can affect us all regardless of our economic or personal circumstances. If you want to get anywhere in your life you have to learn to channel that anger in a way that will help and not hurt you or other people. Be responsible for your own anger, don't take it out on other people or blame them for causing it. Use it to do something good with your life, something that makes you happy and fulfilled. If you are angry at your circumstances and don't feel you get enough help then go out and ask for it. There are people everywhere who will help you, if you want to get good at anything you will find, if you try someone who can train you and start you on the road you want to travel.

Anger has been very helpful to me in my life. I would go as far saying that being bullied was the best thing that ever happened to me. I honestly believe that I would not be enjoying the great life I have today without moving house and schools aged twelve. Without the anger that being bullied gave me I don't think I'd have had the motivation to do as well as I have. Without it I may not have made it to university in Leeds, got a great degree and had the time of my life ever since.

Being bullied and having to rebuild my confidence again taught me that I can do anything I want too. Nothing can ever be as hard as that four or so years at school. Feeling so much fear, being put down so much and thinking the whole world was against me. The whole experience gave me the courage and determination to do everything I want too. Of course I still feel fear at new challenges but it's more a sense of excitement than of not wanting to do it. I feel I've already wasted enough time living in fear so I'm just going to go out and do the things I want too.

I'm not ever going to stop myself doing something in case it doesn't work out, I'll do it regardless. I know because of being bullied that I won't ever sit down aged 65 and kick myself for not talking to that girl I like. For not taking that round the world trip, for not going for that job I

want but don't think I can get... I'm going to go out and
do it regardless of any fear.

Chapter 16

'So Called 'Fighters'

At every school there's one lad who's acknowledged as the best fighter, my school was no different. I once remember our resident 'hard man' punching a lad who was no physical threat to him so hard he broke his cheekbone. Afterwards he was sure to tell all the girls that it wasn't even his hardest punch. **It saddens me that this impresses some people**. This lad was acknowledged as the hardest in our school (though acknowledged by both the headmaster and later a magistrate as an absolute waste of space.) A slight contradiction there I feel. Rather like Prince George in Blackadder acknowledging himself as a great moral and spiritual leader and being acknowledged by almost everyone else as a fat, flatulent git!

Bullies are not strong people. They may be aggressive. They may even be able to fight well and hit hard but that's the only reason they're perceived to be strong. Their approach to life and the people they meet will never bring them lasting respect or admiration from the people who matter. You don't win a person's friendship with a closed fist. The bullies who hit hard are respected only because they are feared. Being afraid of someone does not allow you to like him or her. Making someone afraid of you also does not allow you to be liked.

In my opinion the strong people in life, those who are worthy of respect and admiration are those who have the courage to be nice and to help others. The strong people in life have the self-confidence and esteem within themselves to know that everyone is a friend. Strive to be one of life's strong people. Have courage in the face of fear and you will avoid being a victim. Have the strength to rise above your ego and insecurity and you will avoid becoming a bully.

Fighting

Fighting? What a waste of time that is. People will fight over anything, often the pettiest, most insignificant things. Certainly in every school there's at least one person who will fight at the drop of a hat. In every pub (when you're old enough to go to the pub!) you always encounter the divvy who has one pint or seven too many and says, 'What the fuck are you looking at?' These people do cause big problems in society and I guess it's a case of answers on a postcard as to how to deal with them. But I would advise you to avoid them, don't waste any of your time getting into a conversation with them.

A good motto that will make your life a lot easier and happier is this 'A fight avoided is a fight won.' I really dislike fighting and especially dislike people with a 'must fight' mentality. I encountered a lot of people like that at school and i remember one story in particular. I was sixteen and sitting my GCSE history exam. It got to the end of the exam and the teachers started letting everyone leave in rows. It got to my row and the one next to me and I stood up, at exactly the same time the lad opposite me got to his feet. Obviously keen to leave we bumped into each other, 'wanker' he said. I got that familiar feeling of being under attack so I walked off. I got outside and heard his voice behind me; again he called me a 'wanker'. I turned around and found him standing ready to fight me. After a few years of meeting people like him I wasn't shocked that he wanted to fight me because I'd bumped into him. But I just walked away because I knew who the real 'wanker' was.

So please don't be concerned about people thinking you a 'coward' or a 'wimp' for not fighting, just walk away from them. Whilst we're on the subject, why are so many people afraid of being called those two words? Who cares if someone thinks you're a 'wimp' or a 'coward' because you don't choose to spend your time fighting. I don't care if someone thinks me a wimp because I'll still avoid societies so called 'fighters' every chance I get. I say if they really want to fight they should get down to a good boxing club or do a similar sport where the training is very hard, yet organised and safer than fighting on the streets. If these people have something to prove to themselves they should prove it in the boxing ring, on the mat or on the sports field. That's the proper outlet for your aggression.

So yes there is too much violence in the world and there are too many people walking about looking to 'prove themselves' and cause trouble. I wish these sad people would do themselves and the world a favour and drop the violence. It only ruins people's lives in one way or another; it certainly does nothing to improve them. The bullies and troublemakers are actually very weak in my opinion, not hard, because they cannot control their ego's and anger and they have to get into fights.

In the entire time that I was bullied (four years) I remember having just three fights. You generally wouldn't find me swinging punches, encircled by a baying mob. I'd more likely be walking away from someone insulting me and trying to start a fight. Although my confidence has increased dramatically I am still likely to do the exact same thing today. If that makes me a 'wimp', then so be it I couldn't care less what anyone else thinks. Those who were admired or feared at my school were the kids who could hit hard and show the least respect to others. But me I wasn't a fighter, I was a wimp they said.

I knew that I could hit people and get into fights at school. And when people called me a wimp I admit that sometimes I wanted to fight someone just to prove to my antagonists that I really could do it. But I never did do it because it's wrong and it's a waste of time. I remember one kid at junior school who used to wind me up and one day after school he ran past me and had a go at me again. I lost my temper, gave chase and knocked him to the ground. My mum had picked me up from school and she shouted at me to leave this kid alone. I ran back to her and she gave me a telling off and told me that she wasn't bringing me up to be a thug or a bully. From that day I tried not to disappoint her again.

The truth is I don't like fighting and never have. I'd much rather be your friend and tell you a joke than introduce my fist to your face. But the truth is that you have to fight to succeed in life. You have to keep fighting even when everything seems against you. You always need that belief in the closeness of success. But the fight is not with other people; there's no merit in that. 'The fight is with yourself', in your own mind, between your ears. That's where the fight has always been and where it will always be held. The only opponents you have to beat are the thoughts in your head that tell you you're weak and that you can't do what you want too. These are the thoughts that told Rocky Balboa he couldn't beat Apollo Creed. The thoughts that told Arnold Schwarzenegger he couldn't make it as an actor. They're the very same thoughts that tried to tell me I couldn't do so many things that I've since achieved.

I've been fighting these thoughts my whole life and I get stronger every day. While the so-called 'fighters' were encircled in the playground I was in the classroom or the